CONTENT

Introduction   ix
My Disclaimer   xi

Thoughts on My Time in the Army   1
Boot Camp to Vietnam in Six Months   5
Prostitution and the Roll of the Whore   14
Life of a Foot Soldier in The Mongoose   16
The Absolute Tragedy of War   26
First Two Weeks In The Field   28
Fun Time in Vacation Land   40
Back to An Khê, and Civilization   50
The Major Battle of June 21, 1967   53
Fire Fight of July 25, 1967   69
Drank Too Much   83
Company Comes Down With Cholera   88
Wounded by Friendly Fire   92
Battle of The Rock Pile   95
Trouble With Mess Hall Sargent at LZ Pony   104
Central Vietnam Amphibious Assault   110
Fun Day in Bồng Sơn   115
R and R Meeting Jan in Hawaii   127
Punji Stake Wound: Second Purple Heart   130
The Holiday Season 1967   137
Back in the World February 19, 1968   140

Acknowledgments   143
Also By War History Journals   145

MONGOOSE BRAVO VIETNAM

A TIME OF REFLECTION OVER EVENTS SO
LONG AGO

TIMOTHY MCCULLOUGH

Edited by
GRIFFIN SMITH

SGT. TIMOTHY MCCULLOUGH; B CO., 1/5TH 1ST CAVALRY DIV.

APO 96940 VIETNAM

WAS IT WORTH IT?

A TIME OF REFLECTION OVER EVENTS SO LONG AGO

Memoirs of My Days in Arms, Vietnam 9/1966 - 2/1968

"It wasn't me that started that crazy Asian War, but I was proud to go and do my patriotic chore."

— *Ruby, sung by Waylon Jennings, 1966.*

INTRODUCTION

This project has taken me a lot longer than anticipated. I would guess that I've been at it for more than twenty years. It started as a result of wanting to let the mother of a fallen soldier know what happened to her son, as well as where his death took place. She and I had been in contact over the years, during which she asked quite a few questions; so, I began writing it all down. That was the start. This was soon followed by a close Army friend asking me for some information on other events involving our unit. That expanded my written recollection of the Vietnam War.

Most of the soldiers of the Mongoose were young, in their late teens and early twenties. Many volunteered for the Army, but most were drafted. They were just kids, and when given the chance they did kid things.

Once they acclimated to the situation, they now found themselves in and dealt with their own mortality, the fear of the unexpected waned, and they just carried on finding simple pleasures and comforted in the comradeship that developed. In short, they didn't give the horror of it much thought. We all counted the days. Counting forward the numbers of days in-country until you reached the halfway mark of your tour, then you counted days remaining—200, 199, 198 days and a "wake-up" until one goes home. This everybody did. "When you goin' home? 75 and a wake-up"

But what sticks most in my mind is, they were just kids sent to fight someone else's war and, in the process, give up their youth.

MY DISCLAIMER

I've tried to keep this factual, but time has a way of blurring both mind and body. Therefore, at times, I'm not quite sure as to my accounting. Does it reflect how it all took place or is it a reflection, washed by time? I don't know. Please note, it is not a historical accounting. I make no representation that I had privy to all that was going on around me. It reflects only a small insight into a massive array of events. But, as stated, I have tried to keep an accurate accounting.

I question, just who did I write this for? Most probably for myself. It being a way of putting it all to rest. Or, maybe it would have been better not to have started this at all. It did conjure up memories best forgotten. I may have been better served if I had pushed my memories of Vietnam off into the ditch alongside the road traveled and driven on without looking back. In the long run, I believe it has been therapeutic. Therefore, worth the time I put into writing it all down.

I mostly write in the first person, with overuse of I, me, my and so on, but this is also about the large number of fellow soldiers serving right alongside of me. This is as much their story as my own. I should have used the "we," "us," and "together with," a lot more than I did.

We lived, and fought as a unit, covering each other's backs. Most came home to tell their own stories, many didn't. With their memory in mind; *HERE GOES!*

THOUGHTS ON MY TIME IN THE ARMY

I really can't say that I was proud to do my *"patriotic chore"*; probably would rather have stayed home and watched it on television, but go I did. War really isn't for the faint of heart. It is a dirty, nasty business; not at all like that portrayed in Hollywood. The truth being, as an infantryman in a wartime Army, you are nothing more than a pawn on a world chessboard, to be used at will by those who really do not have your best interests at heart. It took many years to finally come to the realization that, in my war, we were nothing more than a walking target. Collectively, we were bait, to get shot at in order for the full might and fury of Uncle Sam's Army to be directed at those doing the shooting. There wasn't anything noble about it.

The Vietnam War was fought as a war of attrition; meaning we could kill more of you than you could of us. Earlier the French tried doing the same. They too failed. I guess in the end we did kill a lot more of them than they did of us, but as with the French, the North Vietnamese still won the war. Even after so many years, it's hard to admit.

I was drafted into Uncle Sam's Army on September 7th, 1966, and was released from active duty two years later, discharged in September 1972. It would be an understatement to say that my time served on active duty was a life-altering two years. Try as I may to convey my emotional state during this time is perhaps reaching too far. In reality, only those who have walked the walk can truly understand the tragedy of those times. Fortunately, I kept a simple journal during my February 1967 through February 1968 tour of duty in the Republic of South Vietnam and will recall, quoting from it as we move along. There are several references in the journal referring to, KIA – Killed in Action – and WIA – Wounded in Action. This type of reference denotes an action committed by the Company or Platoon as a whole, not solely by myself. A few letters were written during this period to my good friend, Bill Simmons, that will also be included for reference. Bill saved these letters and returned them to me many years later.

Soldiers returning home after serving in Vietnam often have differing views on what it was like. The reason for these variations in accounts is probably due to the wide variety of jobs being performed; ranging from cooks to typists, nurses, and orderlies; from keeping inventory and issuing supply, and to maintaining all the varied pieces of equipment, the list of duties just goes on and on. Each person had his own job to do and duties to perform. In addition to that, geography also played a major role in shaping one's opinion. Soldiers who were stationed in the southern delta region of the country fought one type of war; the Marines up on the DMZ (Demilitarized Zone) fought another. Most of my time was spent in and around the Vinh Dinh Province and more precisely the Bồng Sơn plains and Central Highlands, all of which are in the highly populated central coastal region of Vietnam. My official job description was 11 Bravo Infantry Rifleman, more commonly referred to as a grunt, straight leg, or boot. The job boiled down to searching out the enemy wherever he was. Whether in the jungles, villages, mountains or fields, it was our job to engage them up close and personal. It took anywhere from seven to eleven men serving back in the rear of secured areas doing their jobs to keep people, like me, in the fields doing ours.

Most of the time spent in the fields, or perhaps seventy-five percent of it was boring. Twenty percent was us having a good time, followed by being scared the remaining five percent. Within that five percent, fear, mostly of the unknown, would set in motion a strange phenomenon, my adrenalin would take over; this was followed by a state of calm and quite rational thought. The anticipation of the unknown created far more anxiety than was created by the actual events that occurred. Once committed and after the reality of any given situation set in, fear would dissipate. It seemed as though a sixth sense took over once the shooting started. Fear would subside, and instinct would govern one's action. My instincts were generally good. Of course, luck had a lot to do with who survived and who didn't. Unfortunately, the talents honed while in Vietnam have had little commercial value back home in the real world of civilian life.

Within conversations between soldiers, while serving in Vietnam, we often referred to the good old USA as "The World". The reference being that Vietnam was somewhere other than in "the real world." The phrase often uttered being *"they'll never believe this back in the world."* The truth be known, they probably wouldn't.

I was no hero. Utmost in my thinking was self-preservation, followed closely by the welfare of my fellow G.I.s. The thought of giving it all for God and Country never crossed my mind.

It All Began with the Draft

Not so long ago, times were much simpler. With the exception that young men were subject to being drafted into Uncle Sam's Army. During the exuberance of my youth, I really didn't give the draft much consideration, after all, I had made it through my 24th year without so much of an inkling that the draft would ever catch up with me. "No, not me." With the average draft age then being 18 through 22; and me going on 25, I was way too old for the draft, or so I thought.

My wife Jan and I were in our third year of marriage and were finally able to afford our first vacation. It was July of 1966, and with the old VW packed, Jan, Toby our dog, and I were on the open road. First, we headed to Cleveland to visit her sister, then down to Texas to stay a short time with her grandmother. It was there, while in Dallas that my brother Tom was able to run us down with news that a letter from Uncle Sam was awaiting my return. Curiosity of course forced him to open it, confirming the worst; I had been drafted and was ordered to report to the Oakland Induction Center at 7am, on September 7, 1966. Not exactly what I wanted to hear.

Political and popular opposition against the war was just beginning to heat up in the fall of 1966. The news was full of stories sympathetic to draft dodging and running off to Canada. The thought of evading the draft never entered my mind. Running was never a viable option. Not that I was, nor am I, some great patriot. No, it had more to do with obligations and the way I was brought up. I guess my feeling was that it was time for me to do my *"patriotic chore."* So early one morning in September 1966, off to Oakland I went, leaving my beautiful young wife in front of the draft office in Marysville, California, sitting in our one and only possession, our 1963 VW. A world of change, full of unknowns was awaiting us. The short of it being, I would be gone for two years, and Jan would be on her own.

BOOT CAMP TO VIETNAM IN SIX MONTHS

C hance dictated that I was drafted into the Army and not the Marines. It was only a matter of fate which line, and in what row separated my being in the Army or the Marines. To the right, I was a marine. To the left and I was a soldier. One positive came out of the turmoil of the day spent at the Induction Center. I met someone who would become a lifelong friend, Tairl Parks. We managed to spend our whole military career up to and through Vietnam together, seldom separated by more than a few feet.

Parks and I were in the same Basic Training class at Fort Louis in Washington State and Advanced Infantry Training Company in Fort Polk, Louisiana. The same plane took us to Vietnam, landing at the same induction center, assigning us to the same 1st Cav. unit. We were placed in the same Platoon, 3rd, and on the same machine gun crew. For a while, we were in the same hospital at the same time. We knew and still know each other quite well. Up through the time I departed from Vietnam, I probably spent more time sleeping in a fox hole or improvised hooch alongside Parks than I had spent with my wife.

A very strange thing took place upon completion of Basic Training. Those of us assigned to the infantry were to be transported from Fort Louis Washington to Fort Polk Louisiana, to receive advanced training. Approximately 80 fellow soldiers boarded a four-engine, prop propelled plane belonging to Mac V (a U.S-owned air transit company). Midway through our flight, while over the desert of Arizona, the plane suffered a major mechanical failure forcing it to make an emergency landing in the little town of Winslow where we would spend the next three or four days.

"Well, I'm a standing on a corner in Winslow, Arizona and such a fine sight to see. It's a girl, my Lord, in a flatbed Ford slowin' down to take a look at me..."

— *TAKE IT EASY*, THE EAGLES, 1972

We were marched to a motel on the outskirts of town, taking over the entire place. I've often wondered whatever happened to those weary travelers that had previously decided to stay at this motel. Upon arrival, the group was informed that it would be free to go to town and do whatever, but there would be daily musters with mandatory attendance beginning at five p.m. then again at midnight, three a.m. and eight a.m. The order of the day was you will be there and accounted for or else. Advice was given to watch out for the local gentry that probably wouldn't take it too kindly if we were to pursue the local town beauties. *"Be careful and use your head,"* was our parting advice. Parks and I were at once off in search of a bar. Having been locked up in training for over two months, a beer and shot of Old Crow sounded good.

The first bar found was in the dead center of town, on the corner of two main streets. Inside were a couple of gruff-looking old-timers and a few other nefarious looking characters. We soon had our beers and shots of whiskey stacked up in front of us. Being financially challenged with probably no more than twenty dollars between us and not wanting to blow our meager holdings, we downed our drinks and politely asked for the check. Whereupon the bartender looked up with a scowl upon his face and responded: "Your money is no good in here."

We took this to mean that he wanted us out and that the shit was about to hit the fan, but to our surprise, he went on to tell us that whatever we wanted would be on the house, and the bar would always be open to us. We had completely misread the situation and soon found out the whole town was open to us. I guess that word of what had happened, and our being infantry destined for Vietnam had spread throughout the town. We thanked our patron and stepped out onto the corner sidewalk facing the only traffic light for miles.

Yes, we were *"standing on a corner in Winslow Arizona"* when such a strange sight we did see. A parade of vehicles was coming down the street led by what, I don't recall, but it could have been a flatbed Ford? I do recall there being an older convertible, occupied by a guy and a couple of girls. "Get aboard," they shouted, which we did, and away we went for the next three days and nights. Now you tell me, for I do believe that it must have been one of our group that was either involved with the Eagles, a friend or a songwriter, that was standing with us on that corner of Winslow Arizona on that day in late October 1966. Could it have been this encounter that made its way into the journals of Rock & Roll iconic history, immortalized by the Eagles song *Take It Easy*? Right or wrong, I choose to believe so.

We spent the rest of our stay in Winslow being fed in private homes and ushered to all the local sights (*Painted Desert, Petrified Forest, etc...*). We didn't spend a dime and had the time of our lives. The three o'clock a.m. muster was a true "such a sight to see." Out would pile all the soldiers, who then stood at attention while dressed in all States of attire. At the same time hordes of the local kids, boys and girls alike, would pile out of the rooms and stand at each side of the formation of soldiers, patiently awaiting the muster to end and the party to resume. This went on the entire time spent in Winslow. Unfortunately, all good times have a way of ending all too soon, and we soon found ourselves in Fort Polk, located in Shreveport,

Louisiana. I have often wondered if Winslow suffered a population explosion nine months following our departure.

Upon my completion of advanced infantry training and before leaving for Vietnam, I was granted thirty days of leave, which was spent at home with Jan. During what may well have been the last time I would ever see home; I came down with the measles. Could you believe it? What a bummer! It was, by this time, starting to sink in, the reality of my situation was I was going to war, and there loomed a real possibility I would not return. The odds were on my side, but it was still something I had to learn to accept. GET OVER IT —WHAT IS, IS.

Thirty days later Parks and I found ourselves being ushered onto a flight out of Travis Air Force Base, California bound for Tan Son Nut Air Base located just outside of Saigon in the Republic of South Vietnam. My first emotion upon arrival in this vacation land of South East Asia was that I had arrived in a surreal, forbidding world, with a feeling of forlorn, doom.

Upon exiting the plane, one was struck by the heat. It was hot, humid, and full of the smell of burning waste of all description, including human. All the newly arrived G.I.s were herded to an open shelter some 100 yards from where we landed; the new arrivals at one end of a pole barn draped coffins at the other. Some greeting, *"yet for the grace of God go you."* We just stood, with not a word spoken, watching as those draped coffins were loaded into the same plane, we had just departed.

WELCOME TO VIETNAM

There is an abundance of standing and waiting in the Army, and this was no exception. Finally, we were loaded onto a bus that resembled those used here in the States to transport prisoners from jail to jail. It was OD (*olive drab the Army's favorite color*), windows darkened and covered with a metal mesh. One soon understood the reason for the mesh. It was there to stop some bad guy from throwing an explosive device into the bus.

A short ride later, we arrived at the transfer station for new arrivals. From this location, each G.I. is assigned to a unit. The process takes a few days, and there is nothing to do but sit around awaiting your fate. Parks and I put our time to good use perfecting our Pinochle game. We developed a bidding process which enabled each of us to get a pretty good idea what the other was holding. It was similar to the bidding process used in Bridge. We seldom lost. Actually, we never lost, and beer money was easily made.

Parks was assigned and shipped out first to Camp Radcliff in An Khê, the home of the 1st Cavalry. While watching his departure, my thought was that our time together had come to an end, and we would probably never see one another again. (*Parks argues this point with me. He believes it was I who departed first. But either way it makes no difference. We both ended up at the same place.*) A day later I too was sent to the receiving area of the 1st Cav. There, upon my arrival, stood Parks. "Hi Mac," was about all that was said. From here we were assigned to our company. As chance would have it, both Parks and I drew B Company, $1/5^{th}$ Cav.

We didn't know it at the time, but B, 1st of the 5th, had recently lost several boys and needed replacements. In short order, we, along with a few other guys, were standing in the company day room and being assigned to platoons. Again, fate prevailed, placing both of us in the 3rd Platoon.

A Member of the Brotherhood of Mongoose Bravo

Our newly assigned Company was due in from the field (*the reference to the field denotes being out in the hinterland of Vietnam, fighting the war*) in a couple of days for a stand-down (*rest time*), so we were not immediately sent out to join them. Instead, we awaited their arrival back at Base Camp in An Khê. We took advantage of this free time, and in short order, we were off to town (*the hamlet of An Khê*) to check out the infamous Sin City.

The best way to describe Sin City is by forming a mental picture of Tijuana, Mexico condensed into one square block. During the

French War it served as a walled citadel. Somewhere around 1965, it was transformed into the pleasure capital of South Vietnam; with a gated entrance originally guarded by armed U.S. MPs. The streets were lined with bars, brothels, bars that were brothels, a few souvenir stands, and more bars and brothels. It was one big whore house. Horse-drawn pony carts hauled drunken soldiers from one end to the other, circling the interior corridor of the place which was laid out in a manner resembling a racetrack. Buildings blanketed both sides along with other buildings, forming an internal island. Parks, being a Texas boy, didn't take long to discover the Texas Club; so, in we went.

Sin City, at the time, was under the operational control of the U.S. military. Army MPs patrolled the streets, and Army doctors regularly checked the girls for VD. If they passed inspection, they were given a card and stamped on their ass 100% U.S. prime. No card, no work, in Sin City. This all came to a stop following an article, I believe in Look Magazine, spelling out the way American youth was being corrupted.

A couple of days later the company arrived in An Khê, and the troops were at once given free time. Most of the returning men soon found themselves in Sin City along with us new recruits. It was no doubt one of the most fun-filled few days I had while in Vietnam. These guys were full of hell, piss, and vinegar; drinking, carousing, and more drinking.

The new guys were at once welcomed with open arms into their new brotherhood. We were now fully-fledged members of Mongoose Bravo, 1/5th Cavalry, and as such, we were told and actually believed that "you can walk through the valley of the shadow of death, and fear no evil, for now you are one of the meanest sons-of-bitches in that valley." The valley referred to being the Bồng Sơn Plains, a place I would call home for some time. Mongoose Bravo had well earned its reputation as being a "pee bringing outfit."

Unfortunately, all things fun must come to an end. In this case, the end was brought about by just a little misunderstanding while in Sin City, which contributed to the whole company being kicked out of Base Camp and shipped back into the boonies. One of the real downers of Army life was that those in charge lacked a sense of humor. For whatever reason, I was not with the boys on this day, and there are two versions of just what transpired. One was told to me sometime later as part of end-of-day fox hole chatter. The second was an account provided by my good friend Buzzy Suman who took part in the action. (*Buzzy's version is at the end of this chapter*) Fox hole stories grow with each telling; I'm therefore more inclined to believe Buzzy's accounting; however, either way, it's a good story.

It seems, as retold in the fox hole version, that some of our guys shanghaied a couple of the pony carts and were racing them around the internal roadway of Sin City. In Buzzy's version* he, together with Sgt. Troval, was carousing whore houses and partaking in the pleasures of the day when they were accused of not paying off all their debts. They were accused of trying to skip out. This resulted in Sgt. Troval punching and dropping a brothel owner. Upon getting up, he ran out of the establishment and summoned the MPs. Either way, we choose to accept what happened up to this point the MPs put a stop to the pony cart races, or they didn't respond to the punched brothel owner's cry for help—the results are the same.

MPs did intervene, placing a member of the Mongoose under arrest and taking him to a detention area in or adjacent to Sin City. At this point the MPs made a fatal mistake, they turned their back on the rest of the Company that had gathered. In the fox hole version, the MPs stepped into a small booth, or shack, to make a call for back up. This resulted with those gathered tipping over the shack, trapping the MPs inside. While in Buzzy's version, Sgt. Troval is being held in a gated detention holding pen, and Sgt. Veith, our Plt. Sgt. shanghaied a vehicle and used it to ram the gate of the detention holding pen, freeing Sgt. Troval. In both versions, the escape was swift and complete.

The reprisal of the MPs was even swifter. Even before our guys could beat it out of Sin City and back to the Company Area, our Company Commander had been informed of their antics. The next morning helicopters awaited us, and off we went to war. Evidently the brass was really pissed. We were kept out in the jungle, away from any sort of civilization for about three months. I, as previously stated, was not there as these events unfolded.

However, I was present as the Company Commander dressed down the entire Company. More likely than not, a blend of both accounts took place. Some of the guys were racing pony carts, while at the same time Sgt. Troval got a little out of control. Regardless MPs were called in, and one of the Mongoose was put in the hoosegow, whereupon the boys got him out, and the rest was history.

Letter from Buzzy Suman addressing the actions that transpired that day:

2019

Mac,

The following is my recollection of the Sin City incident. Now keep in mind I'm old, and my memory could be a bit cloudy. Anyway, this is how I remember it. It was my second tour of Sin City, and my last. I was with Sgt. Trovoh and someone else I don't remember.

We were seeing how many girls we could have. One drink and one girl and we would go on to the next house of pleasure. Somewhere along the line we didn't pay for a round of drinks or girls or both really by mistake. We were confronted by the Papasan of one of the houses that we had left.

Truth be said, we did pay and punched the Papasan, knocked him on his ass actually and we went on our way. As we were proceeding some MPs and Papasan came and confronted us. We got in a fight with them, and we were doing alright until one of them called for reinforcements. They subdued us, handcuffs and everything. They loaded the three of us in the back of one jeep, and another followed, and they took us to the gatehouse.

Our whole company was down there, and I remember them yelling and asking what's going on and stuff. Anyway, they had us in the gatehouse for 5-10 minutes when someone crashed a jeep through the double door. It was Sgt. Watkins and a bunch of other guys. We took over the gatehouse, and our guys got keys and uncuffed us. After that there was a lot of yelling and confusion.

There was probably 40-50 of us, and the MPs kind of gave up. While all this was going on the Capt. of the MPs showed up, and he was trying to make some order out of this mini riot, but not doing too well. Then our CO. arrived and calmed everything down. At least we listened to him. He got us to leave. I remember thinking we got away with that one, but too soon found out we were getting kicked out of An Khê and going back out to the field.

I always thought it was so cool how Watkins got us out. It was like some movie or something. All the guys came with Watkins leading the charge. We really thought we were hot shit invincible. Maybe some days we were.

That's how I remember it, but I can't remember the third guy.

Your friend,
Buzzy Suman

PROSTITUTION AND THE ROLL OF THE WHORE

In writing this, I often refer to the Vietnamese women of the night. Sure, they were all whores, but they were so much more. They were the only social female contact available to the average guy, and they would sit with you for hours and just talk. Especially if one was buying beer. No beer led to a shorter conversation. If the G.I.s wanted something more, they would provide it. However, it wasn't necessary. If you were buying beer, they and the madam they worked for, were happy—money was being made. While I was able to refrain from bedding them, I sure did drink a lot of beer with them. This was how I spent my time when in Sin City, talking to the working girls while my young compatriots disappeared into the back rooms. Friendships were made with certain girls, and they would break away from another G.I. if she saw you entering the establishment. I was able to learn quite a bit about the Vietnamese culture from them, and they a lot about the USA from me. I found it interesting that many had families and were often married. Some were sold into the profession, others entered into it on their own to support their extended families, including their mothers, fathers, grandparents, and siblings. They seemed to accept their station in life and carried on as best as they could. Strange isn't it, a person being sold and just accepting it. I learned early in my tour not to judge the Vietnamese. They lived by their own social canons, not ours.

Please, don't take this to mean that the Vietnamese have a low moral character, for on the most part that's not the case. Overall, the Vietnamese are quite moral with strict taboos regarding sexual interaction. Girls under the age of eighteen, which was assumed to be the age of consent, were closely watched. One seldom encountered a young, teenage girl while patrolling the countryside. The Vietnamese didn't trust us. The villagers were led to believe we were all rapists; therefore, they hid their daughters, and only on rare occasions did we encounter a young girl. I know of no time that a G.I. forced himself on any of those encountered. But that is what the VC had led the villagers to believe, and they took no chances. In population centers, girls freely roamed the streets; that is except for girls high on the social scale, which could be recognized by the manner of their dress (*long black hair in a ponytail, black silk pajama pants and white silk blouse that hung almost to their knees*). When you did see one of these girls, they were generally walking away or crossing the street to steer clear of you. Eye to eye contact was always avoided. Overall, the Vietnamese protected their young women from G.I.s.

LIFE OF A FOOT SOLDIER IN THE MONGOOSE

I believe it appropriate at this juncture to offer a window into the average day of the infantryman serving in my platoon. The truth is, there really wasn't such a thing as an average day. Each day offered up a verity of unique challenges, but some things remained forever the same, such as what did we wear, carry, drink, and eat? Where did we sleep and how much sleep did we get each night? How would we get resupplied and/or bathe? Much of daily life did follow a tedium of routine. To begin with, we seldom bathed, perhaps getting wet all over not more often than every three or four weeks. I guess we really smelled, but one gets used to it. It is my contention that a man only smells for a few days following the taking of a bath. After that the smell seems to go away. As for the daily grind, we were generally up and about shortly after daylight. There was limited time devoted to taking down your hooch, gathering up your gear and in general getting ready for the day's trek through Oz. Both water and free time were scarce, so washing, shaving, and dental hygiene were most often forgotten. One didn't have to dress because we slept fully clothed in our fatigues and boots, both of which were never off until they rotted off. Then new fatigues and boots would be flown in as part of the regular resupply for the Company. We never wore underwear;

however, many did wear undershirts. As for our general appearance, it was pretty "ragtag."

As stated, we were in our boots day and night. We slept in them; never taking them off until a new pair was furnished, which happened about every month or so. We wore socks and jungle boots which, as stated, were never taken off, not until being furnished a replacement. Then one actually peeled off the socks that had become attached to the dead skin of your foot. Considering this lack of attention to foot care, you would think that foot rot would have been a serious problem, but neither I nor anyone else that I can recall suffered serious foot problems.

The early morning was devoted to readying oneself for the day's mission. Often breakfast would be flown in, and we could look forward to hot coffee, powdered eggs, bacon, and bread. If a hot meal wasn't flown in, a can of C-rations was opened. We prayed for the hot meal. Following breakfast, usually at about seven, we put on our packs which contained everything of a personal nature we possessed, as well as, everything needed for our survival and mission. It all had to be carried: weapons and ammo, grenades, claymore mines, trip flares, machetes, ponchos, mosquito nets, extra C-rations, entrenching tools, personal items, and as much water as one could carry. The average load per soldier was probably well over fifty pounds. To this I had the additional burden of carrying the platoon radio, together with its extra battery and various other paraphernalia, adding twenty-six or so pounds. I would estimate that my entire load was about seventy to eighty pounds. This was hauled day in and day out, over the mountains, jungles, and through the villages of Vietnam. Periodically, but certainly not part of the norm, a helicopter carrying a wire basket would be loaded with our packs, which would be returned once we had arrived at our new bivouac area. This practice was referred to as "going light." All that we carried when "going light" was our weapons, a poncho, machete, ammo, water, Cs, and of course the radio, thus lightening our load considerably.

It's hard to estimate how many miles we walked during my tour. Sometimes the walking was easy, as when we were in the valleys and villages. The mountains were another story. They were steep, dry, and covered with thick brush, bamboo, high elephant grass, and overhead tree canopy. Each bush had thorns, the grass offered up a thousand paper cuts, but it was the overhead tree canopy that created the biggest threat. It separated us from being able to be observed by air support. Because of this cloaking of ground activity, I came to believe it was an often-used hiding place for the enemy. Find overhead canopy, water, both of which near a populated area and chances where you would find Charlie.

Hacking through thick jungle and making only two to three thousand meters per day was not uncommon; however, ten to fifteen clicks were probably the norm. Critters of all descriptions were always trying to hitch a ride, especially in the rivers and streams which were infested with leeches. They attached themselves to your skin and sucked blood, swelling to about the size of a finger, but didn't hurt. It was more the idea of them being there. All in all, it was hot, dirty, nasty work.

About every two weeks or so, a box, referred to as a summary would be dropped in. The summaries contained personal items needed for hygiene, such as toothpaste, soap, razors, blades, and toilet paper, as well as comfort items such as Hershey candy bars that wouldn't melt, lifesavers (we traded for the cherry and yellow ones), and cigarettes. Having the summaries dropped in was a big deal. Guys would grab what they needed, and trade for what they wanted. On rare occasions, warm beer and soda would accompany the drop. An enlisted man is entitled to a ration of two beers per day. Of course, this never happened, but on occasion, beer did arrive. Some of the boys would rather have the soda pop that accompanied the beer drop, so a lot of trading took place. Me, I gathered all the beer I could manage to get my hands on, buried it down deep in my pack and awaited the day when a beer would really be appreciated. Because of the additional weight associated with these canned beverages and other canned goods, most of the boys preferred to only take what they could consume on the spot and trade away what they decided not to carry. Cigarette trading was a major undertaking. Cigarettes were not only contained in the summaries but, a package of four various brands was part of our daily C-rations. Of course, each soldier had his favored brand. No one wanted the Kents; therefore, these were readily available (*Marlboro, Winston, and Salem being the favored brands*). I would gather all the discarded Kents I could and stash them away, knowing that somewhere along the way we would get into a firefight. During these times, cigarettes were consumed in large volume, making my hoarded Kents something of high value as the boys ran out of their brands. I gave the Kents out to those who had diminished their supply. Fortunately for me, I had a strong back and could carry the extra weight of my hold out stash.

A briefing was held each morning during which we would be informed as to where we would be going, if enemy activity could be expected, and if we would be operating at platoon strength (twenty to thirty men, most often closer to twenty) or as part of the whole company (a hundred to a hundred and twenty or so). Although a little scary, due to the reduced number of G.I.s committed to the patrol, I nevertheless, preferred patrolling at the reduced platoon strength due to the solitude and independence of being away from the company and being masters of our own fate. Following the morning briefing, we readied ourselves for the daily mission, which usually involved undertaking yet another search and destroy patrol. By this I mean, looking for the bad guy, having him shoot at us and engaging him. We departed our previous night's bivouac area by either walking or boarding helicopters and air assault into a new location. We seldom, if ever spent two nights in the same area. When flying in by helicopter, one never knew what the terrain would be like until jumping out and landing on solid ground.

Most of the time, choppers could land, but often they could not. On more than a few occasions, tall grass (elephant grass) obscured both the pilot, as well as those of us about to unload a view of the ground upon which we would land. In these conditions, one had to just leap, not knowing the distance one would be falling. All we could do was wait for the landing. The fall could be a couple of feet, or it could be much more. The ground we were about to land on could be composed of soft dirt, low hanging brush, or we could be landing on a bunch of rocks. We never knew for sure until hitting the ground. What we did know was that the jolt would be horrific. These leaps of faith could also occur when being inserted into a hot Landing Zone (LZ). By this I mean the chopper would be inserting us into an LZ that was already under fire. In which case the chopper would slow down and momentarily hover a foot or two over the ground, and we would jump and often tumble. The chopper making his exit while we were still in the process of jumping. I, to this day, believe, and the VA has confirmed, that to a great extent my back and other skeletal problems can be attributed to those leaps of faith. Remember, I had seventy to eighty pounds on my back when I hit the ground. Thud and then, fifty years later knee, back, shoulder and neck problems.

The daily search and destroy patrol involved walking until about noon, at which time a halt was called, and a can of Cs would be consumed. After a short rest, we were off again, not stopping until a couple of hours before the sunset. If by chance we did happen to encounter the enemy, it was usually by accident. But when it happened, all hell could break loose. They would shoot at us. We would shoot back. We would follow up by trying to disengage, pulling back to allow the firepower of the United States to be unleashed upon them. Artillery would pound the suspected enemy position, after which, we would go back and probe the area. If shooting erupted again, then the whole process was repeated. The idea was to make a target of ourselves, engage, and then pull back, allowing the place to be blown to hell. Now that's the true definition of a "Search and Destroy Mission." This type of contact was usually limited in scale, but we never knew. On occasion, it could turn out to be a real humdinger. We could anticipate making enemy contact when patrolling in a mountainous area with overhead canopy, adjacent to water and relatively close to an inhabited area or in a village adjacent to mountains with cover and water.

If not engaged in a search and destroy mission, we would probably be in actual pursuit of a known, or perceived, target, or coming to the aid of another sister company already engaged. Pursuing a suspected enemy usually panned out to be nothing more than a long walk. Coming to the aid of another American unit already engaged was different; it was scary. You knew that in short order, you'd be in it. I personally found this the most sobering of situations. The anticipation of an upcoming firefight could rattle the nerves of the most hardened soldier. We hoped and prayed that the shooting would be over before we got there; generally, that was the case, but often it wasn't. You just never knew.

On a few occasions, and these were by far my favorite, involved going out in small numbers of five or six people. We would go into a suspected, enemy-held area, or transit area, and sneak around until we found a well-camouflaged spot that afforded plenty of viewing area. This type of mission was referred to as a LRRP patrol; LRRP meant Long Range Recon Patrol. We would stay huddled up in our hiding place, observing. We weren't expected to engage unless we were discovered. If that were to happen, we were to run like hell until we could be extracted. Thank God we were never discovered. LRRPs lasted no more than five or six nights. The only real hang-up was running out of food and water, which did happen on one occasion, which I will discuss later.

At the end of a normal day, a new bivouac area would be found, and new defensive positions established. Fox holes were dug, and our hooch erected (*A hooch is a tent-like structure made by the joining together of two or more ponchos*). Claymore mines and trip flairs were put in place about twenty to thirty meters to the perimeter's front.

Digging the fox hole, followed by the constructing of a hooch could happen simultaneously, with part of the guys devoted to digging the fox hole and others dedicated to erecting the nightly hooch, while yet others put in place the night security, consisting of setting out trip flares and claymore mines. If lucky, a hot meal and water would be flown in, or else another can of C-rations would be offered up. Most of the time, but not always, a listening post or night ambush patrol would be sent out.

Each fox hole could accommodate three or four soldiers. From this number, a nightly guard rotation would be established, leaving at least one person awake, and on guard in each hole throughout the night. Each person was expected to take his turn as part of this rotation. As one would come off guard, he would awaken his replacement and then take over his replacement's place in the hooch. This strange dance was carried out night after night. To make sure no one slept on guard, a common watch was passed from the person on guard to the person replacing him. In this manner, the watch would eventually be passed to the last person on guard in the morning. If there was a foul-up or someone went to sleep the person still holding the watch was guilty. This rotation would go on through the night, with each soldier knowing that he would be rousted from sleep twice and would be spending two-plus hours on guard. As a result, the normal amount of sleep one could expect was between five and a half, to six hours, making sleep deprivation a serious, but a necessary problem. Because the same guys shared the same hole and hooch each night, a strong bond was formed, and a kinship developed.

In the evenings, just before sunset, and after eating a meal, social interaction took place. C-ration coffee would be brewed by combining within a canteen cup, a packet of sugar, instant coffee, creamer, and powdered hot chocolate. This was then heated over a makeshift can stove fueled by either heat tabs, or with a small piece of C4 explosive that was extracted from a claymore mine. This mixture would be passed around among those gathered. Stories of first love, home life, families, or the last bought and paid for Vietnamese boom-boom girl would be discussed in detail. There was little that we didn't know about each others' families, hometowns, relationships, likes, and dislikes. Stories were told and retold. Often songs, yes guys did sing, would be sung and passages from books recited. My friend Parks had a good country western voice, and he serenaded us nightly, "Frankie and Jonnie" was a favorite. He was also able to recite verbatim the *"Burring of Sam Magee,"* as well as the one about the *"Stigmatizing Monkey."* The bonds established during these evening hours were extremely strong and have lasted throughout my life.

As for the hooch itself, as stated, these were merely two ponchos snapped together and stretched end to end with two poles holding up each end. A cord was attached to the top of each pole and then staked to the ground. On occasion, a ridge pole was attached to the upright poles adding strength to the nightly quarter. The upright poles and occasional ridge poles were sticks we gathered each evening; the ponchos were staked down at the four corners. Often a third poncho was thrown over the opening at one end. The troops took quite a bit of pride and used a lot of imagination in individualizing the construction of their nightly hooch.

Air mattresses were inflated by lung power; one for each sleeping place. (*Our air mattresses were quite narrow, maybe twenty inches, and no more than four to five foot long.*) That meant one of the group wouldn't have to blow up his mattress. All manner of games and tricks were employed to be the one relieved from air mattress inflating duty. New guys were always tricked into blowing up the entire group. After which laughter could be heard. Mosquito netting was hung inside which offered some protection from the nasty pests, but I believe that the netting ensnared more mosquitoes inside than were flying around outside. If you happened to erect your hooch over some form of creepy crawler, you would undoubtedly find it out in the middle of the night and have to share your quarters with it.

When in known highly hostile areas, a low-profile hooch was constructed. The top of which was no more than a foot or so off the ground, thus making it extremely difficult to distinguish from the surrounding jungle floor. If in a really hostile area, no hooch would be constructed, and we slept as best as we could, unprotected from the elements. A G.I. could sleep anywhere, anytime, and under any condition.

Procuring water in adequate quantities could be extremely difficult. We constantly ran out of it. One would think that in a wet, humid country like Vietnam, water would be plentiful. It wasn't. When patrolling mountain tops, it was extremely scarce, only available in running streams as we moved down into the ravines and valleys. Of course, this was also a problem for the bad guys who didn't have the luxury of being resupplied by air. We could anticipate an attempt would be made to fly in water, but on occasion, for whatever reason, this didn't happen. I recall, on one occasion we had to gather up all the water each soldier was carrying and ration it out. An attempt was made to drop water to us, but unfortunately, most of the water bladders that dropped burst upon hitting the ground. Couple this with the eating of C-rations, which are high in salt, and we had a problem. We did eventually get a resupply of water later the next day.

When water was available at stream crossings or when we came upon a well, we employed *Halazone* tablets as a means of purifying the water we collected in our canteens. They must have worked. Except for one occasion, I don't believe I suffered from a water-borne disease; even though my canteen was sometimes filled with rice patty water. The amount of water each soldier carried was dictated by his anticipated need and ability to carry the extra load. Me, I carried a lot, usually a gallon, plus.

Here's the low down on C-rations, the breakfast of champions. They are a meal contained within a can and in a box containing a variety of offerings. There were three basic groupings *(B-1, B-2, & B-3)* with each group containing several different meals. While there were a variety of offerings, the choices that were offered within the group were always the same. Within the B-2 group you will always find an offering of ham and eggs. A B-3 group would always contain a box of ham and limas. And within the boxes from each group were the same supplements. For example, one could expect to find a can of cheese spread in a meal from the B-3 group. From another group, you may find a packet of powdered chocolate drink. In all, there were probably a couple dozen or more specific offerings. Each box, regardless of group, would contain toilet paper, four cigarettes, paper napkin, and knife and fork. We knew what could be found within the variety of meals offered and reached for a specific meal box when given an opportunity. The one staple supplement used to enhance the meal but not provided within the box was Tabasco Hot Sauce. A lot of soldiers carried their own bottle.

It appeared no one wanted ham and limas except for me. They were contained in a larger can that was bulky and heavier than the average meal. We always tried to limit the weight we had to carry; therefore, most didn't want to carry ham and limas. Because of this and the fact that no one liked them, made them readily available. My formula for making them palatable required opening the can from the bottom, removing a portion of the fatty ham and replacing it with cheese spread and peanut butter. Both supplements were offered in other C-ration meals. It was pretty good.

THE ABSOLUTE TRAGEDY OF WAR

D eath, pain, and suffering were a constant companion for those foot soldiers who actually fought the war. The soldier often questioned his immortality and dealt with the fact that he may not be going home. The inner scars of Vietnam would be carried for life. It can never be completely eradicated from one's inner soul. Some cope, the less fortunate find it more difficult.

Let's address this issue, upfront before I get into discussing various firefights and shoot-em-ups. Would I try to kill another human? How would I react to seeing men shot and hurt? Would I be able to control my emotions? Of course, these were concerns; but concerns soon answered in a very short span of time in the jungles of Vietnam.

James Fennimore Cooper once so wisely foretold in his *The Leather Stocking Tales* spanning the 1740-1806 of early American exploration, that one could watch the full humanity of man in a short period of time digress back to his savage roots when first he left the comforts of the eastern seaboard to explore, then trap and hunt the lands west of the Alleghenies. Then finally he would regain his civility as he settled the regions west of the Cumberland Gap.

I doubted that man could so digress and then recapture humanity in such a short period of time. But Cooper was right. I believe that we each have an inherent capability residing within us that allows us to do unthinkable things. The trick, the one we will be judged by, is how well we control this beast. When someone tries to kill you, if given a chance, you will kill them. When shot at, you will shoot back. You will learn to detach yourself from witnessing the unthinkable. When a buddy is hurt, you will dress his wound and try to comfort him.

For me, Vietnam was my Cumberland Gap. Did I ever shoot somebody? I imagine so. On two separate occasions, I took aim at another human being who was a short distance away and pulled the trigger with full intent on ending a life. Most of the time your rifle is fired at where you suspect the enemy is located. Seldom did I actually see him, place my sight on him, and pull the trigger. So, could I have killed an enemy soldier—probably, but not sure. I didn't wait around to find out. Did I fully intend, given the opportunity, to kill enemy soldiers? Yes. Do I now feel remorse for doing it? I accept the contradiction of values it created. It was war and given the opportunity they would have surely killed me, but as time goes by feelings do change. Deep down, now, I guess I would rather have missed, but I won't lose sleep over it. I did it, and that's just the way it was. We were there to kill and not be killed. Did innocent people die? Yes.

In the end, I crossed the Cumberland Gap into the wilderness, and in due time came back home to civilization. In doing so, I tamed the beast. I fully understand that God, not man, will be the final arbiter of my actions, and I willingly await his judgment. Now that's over, the elephant's out, and we will discuss these things no more. In the end, time washes all wounds.

FIRST TWO WEEKS IN THE FIELD

FROM MY JOURNAL

March 8th Left An Khê for the field. Flew to English and air assaulted into Tiger Mts.

March 9th Fire Fight Tiger Mountains. 2 WIA (Wounded in Action).

March 10th Marched Up Mountains.

March 11th Extracted & Air Assault into the Newie News.

March 12th Blocking Force—Chow line hit. 1 WIA.

March 21st Fire Fight at Hill 55, Bồng Sơn.

During my first two weeks in the field, several men were wounded; fortunately, there were no fatalities. The dramatic unfolding of those first two weeks quickly transformed me into a veteran combat soldier. I recall talking with one of the veteran sergeants following those horrific two weeks. First, he smiled and assured me that it would not always be like this. Then stated, "You boys sure earned your 'CIB'" (Combat Infantry Badges). The CIB is the badge of distinction, or the infantryman's modern *Red Badge of Courage* and only worn by infantrymen who have survived thirty days of sustained combat. This kind sergeant lost his life on June 21st, just a week before he was scheduled to return home to the States.

The first firefight I was involved in was on the evening of March 9th. The Company, or it could have been the Platoon, had just set up for the night; digging fox holes and setting up our shelters on a knoll located within eyesight of the South China Sea. I had just settled down in the newly erected hooch, and by the light of the fading sun began writing a letter to Jan, explaining to her how beautiful the view was from our small mountain top. It was about this time all hell broke loose. I recall seeing, or more accurately feeling, bullets flashing over my head. They slashed through the poncho which covered the front, top and sides of the hooch. Out I crawled, grabbing my rifle as I made for our fox hole. The machine gun to my right, which was manned by a fellow from New York named Little had already engaged, returning fire, pounding the adjacent hillside. It wasn't long before our Navy, which was stationed off the coast, began sending in high explosive rounds. They kept this up for what seemed like fifteen to twenty minutes, then periodically throughout the night. The night skies were illuminated by aerial flares. When all was finally quiet, I had survived my first firefight. One of the boys to my right was not so fortunate, having been hit several times, one of which I was told took off some fingers. I didn't realize it at the time, but what I had just experienced was actually a minor event.

Four days later, on March 12th, we found ourselves involved in what is best described as a very unusual chain of events, even by Vietnam standards. We set up on a mountain ridgeline to be a blocking force preventing the escape of a bunch of the bad guys who had been trapped in the ravine somewhere below our position by another Company of the 1st Cav. We believed they were quite some distance from our position. Nothing was happening, and it was assumed that they had somehow taken their leave, disappearing into the adjacent jungle. The Company, stretched out along the ridge top, settling in for the night with hot chow being flown in. A chow line was formed, and we were called, a few at a time, to come get hot food. Eventually, it was my turn to get in the chow line. Unfortunately, just as I finished filling my tray, the bad guys, decided to make a break, through our line. They started by throwing grenades, wounding one of my fellow "newbies." Then the shooting started. There I stood food in hand, rifle slung over my shoulder, looking for a place to duck into for protection from the incoming fire. A couple of large rocks were spotted, and I made a dive, not spilling any of my precious hot meal. Unfortunately, the point dog had already claimed this position. What was worse, bristling snarls and barring teeth, or bristling bullets and grenade shrapnel? I chose to relocate, finding another rock to get behind so I could eat my chow, and if the occasion warranted, shoot my M16. Again, misfortune as I landed on a bunch of ants. Sometimes you just can't win. In short order, the ants succeeded in forcing me to reconsider my position and take another course of action. After giving it some thought, I concluded that the best thing for me to do was to try to make my way back to my platoon and foxhole.

Upon taking my leave, I came across a couple of G.I.s hunkered behind a group of large rocks. Looking up, they warned me to duck when running across a little opening that was separating me from my destination. Charlie (*North Vietnamese Army or Viet Cong*) was shooting at everything that passed through this little opening. I had to scoot, with food tray in tow, and rifle in hand, and the pop, pop, popping of bullets buzzing overhead as I cleared the opening. SO, THIS IS THE REALITY OF VIETNAM! In a relatively short period of time, the Army had provided me with hot food, only to be followed by getting shot at, having a grenade thrown at me, a dog trying to bite me, and being eaten alive by ants. Through all of this, I was finally able to finish my meal in relative peace. Hot food could be hard to come by in those days, and worth a little effort in the getting.

I guess one could call the firefights of March 9th and 12th warmups for a main event that came on March 21st. A firefight had sprung up south of both the hamlet of Bồng Sơn and LZ English where we were committed. Our objective was to chase Charlie off a hill, referenced on our maps as Hill 55. It was a real humdinger of a firefight. A sister company was getting hammered, and we were to help by attacking a flank which contained the high ground, Hill 55. We were strung out with our platoon sergeant having us run at intervals, one and two at a time, head-on into incoming enemy fire. I can recall him saying to Parks and me as he ordered us to advance, "Just do as I tell you boys and you'll be all right. When I tap you on the shoulder, run." He did, and we did, running up the hill and cresting its top, firing the whole time, at what, I don't know. Our platoon leader, Lt. Stan Derr, was seriously wounded during the advance, but miraculously he was the only casualty we suffered. He was in short order medevaced back to the forward hospital at LZ English and eventually back home. Fortunately, he lived to tell his grandchildren his story.

Upon reaching the top of the hill, we took up defensive positions, only to be told that we now had to assault down the other side and into a village that Charlie was holding. Again, off we went. The noise was deafening, and bullets were whizzing in all directions, tracers from both sides streaking across the sky. I was running like hell itself was chasing, running next to, but slightly behind Parks as we descended the mountain. I recall seeing a couple of tracers from incoming bullets whizzing, at what looked to be, straight at Park's head. I shouted out to him to make sure he was all right, but somehow, they missed him. The thought then struck me, "if they missed Park's head, just how in the hell did they miss me?" Parks hit the ground behind a small dike that was being used by several of our guys for protection on the outskirts of the village. Just as this was happening, a large burst of enemy fire came from my left flank and slightly to our rear. It's strange, but you can hear a bullet when it barely misses you. It makes a cracking sound, not unlike the snapping of your fingers, as it passes. Hearing these bullets coming from my left rear, I hit the dike and climbed over to the other side for protection. Parks was on one side of the dike, looking at me on the other, shouting "Mac, get back over the dike, they're shooting at you from our front."

In response, I yelled, "What the hell, they're shooting at us from behind too." Go figure, no place to hide.

We made it into the village, or what was left of it and set up for the night without taking any further casualties. That night was spent with Parks and me lying on top of a dirt path within the village; night illumination lighting up the sky. We fully expected a night counterattack, but it never materialized. Somehow, unbeknownst to me, we had succeeded in chasing out the bad guys. It was a long night indeed that followed. Through the haze of the night illumination, one could observe this young woman, not much over her mid-twenties, some seventy-five to one hundred yards to my front, who was trying to salvage what was left of her small thatch home. The next morning on our departure from the burned out village we walked by this poor young soul. She wore a bewildered look on her face and a bandage on her head, no doubt the result of the artillery barrage fired into her village. I would like to believe that one of our medics put on the bandage. She looked up, and I will never forget that look of despair on her face, saying without uttering a word, "why did you do this to me?" as she continued attempting to put out the small fire that had destroyed her home.

That ended my first two weeks in the wilds of the "Disneyland of South East Asia," where nothing was really as it seemed.

Relieving the Marines at Montezuma

For some reason, I didn't write anything in my diary between March 21st and May 17th. During this period, we did see quite a bit of action including the Company relieving Marines located at a landing zone called Montezuma (later referred to as LZ Leon). Montezuma was located close to the hamlet of Duc Pho in the Quang Ngai Provence. Quang Ngai is immediately north of the Binh Dinh Provence and forms the Southern border of "I" Core which separated the Marines' area of operation from that of the Army.

Somewhere around April 7th, we began what was about a ten to fifteen-day sweep, circling about three to five miles out from Montezuma. It was here that I had my first really close call, coming very close to being blown away by a land mine.

We were in constant contact with Charlie the whole time spent in this operation. Nothing really big, just constant snipping and light skirmishes. A whole lot of guys got hurt or saw their last day during this operation. I was becoming quite hardened by this time, feeling little remorse for those getting hurt or killed. I had developed a fatalistic attitude towards the whole affair. However, something was about to happen that would snap me back. We were operating at platoon strength of probably no more than 25 guys, hunting Charlie, when we happened to walk into a VC hospital, prompting a whole lot of Bang, Bang–boom, boom. It came to an end with Charlie fleeing the area and, in the process, leaving behind a small infant, no more than one to two-years-old. No doubt his mother was frantic. Now we had a dilemma, knowing full well that we would be calling in artillery and wiping this place, as well as the surrounding area, off the face of the earth. We couldn't leave the child. He would surely perish if we did. Without discussion, or seeking permission, I picked him up and carried him away with us as we made our departure. I guess I felt a responsibility for this little fellow and wanted him reunited with his family, even though this same family only a short time earlier had tried very hard to kill us all. Once we were a good distance away from where the artillery would land, I was told to put the child down. Which I did, hoping that the baby would be found by his mother, whom we suspected had been keeping an eye on us. I carry that hope with me to this day.

As for the next close encounter, it involved a booby-trapped explosive buried in a trail leading into a village. It transpired just a few days after leaving the infant. The Company was approaching, what we believed to be a relatively large, friendly village when we noticed villagers running out the other side; a sure sign that bad guys were inside. How many were in there? We had no idea, but Charlie was most definitely there. We came up on an assault line, which was reminiscent of what you would see in old Revolutionary War movies, with the British walking abreast, straight into the enemy line of fire. However, in our case we were four to six feet apart and carrying automatic rifles. The effect on the opposing side was overwhelming. We shouted, grunted and snarled, and in most cases, fired our M16s on fully automatic as we advanced. You would think that we'd get the hell shot out of us, but, you know, in the numerous times I was involved in this tactic, we never lost a man. The trick is to keep the line straight so that you're advancing toward the opposing force in one broad assault, firing everything you got, forcing the enemy to keep his head down while one advances. The only difference being, that on this occasion, we were not firing our rifles. Why? Because this village was reported to be pacified, friendly, on our side. We were under orders to only shoot if we are shot at, even if we encountered suspected enemy soldiers carrying weapons. We had to be shot at before we could return fire. What a joke. Someone seriously miscalled this one. But, the order remained, do not shoot unless shot at. The rules of engagement were often implemented in a case such as this, where the Marines had worked with the villagers in securing their loyalty.

We had to cross a large flooded rice field and were in five or six inches of mud as we advanced. On making my way across the field, I happened to be walking adjacent to an elevated footpath running in the same direction, straight into the village. Knowing that it would be a hell of a lot easier to walk on the trail than through the mud, at about thirty yards out, I climbed up onto the path and continued moving forward. It finally occurred to me that I was the only one on this trail, thus making myself a very inviting target. Back into the mud I went. No more than a couple of steps, a really BIG BOOM! I was spun around and knocked to the ground by the concussion of the blast, which occurred no more than fifteen yards from me. I was dazed, maybe unconscious for a few seconds. Charlie, being the mean little bastard he was, had planted an unexploded 105 artillery round in the trail and, because he was being pressured by our advance, was forced to prematurely detonate it with a hand device just before I was on top of it. His mistake and my saving grace were that he buried the 105 round too deep in the trail; thus, the blast carried its shrapnel up and over my head. All I suffered was the concussion of the explosion. One of the sergeants and another fellow walking behind the assault line were not so lucky and were hit by shrapnel. I was a little shell shocked but unhurt. It was a really close call and as I think back on it, GOD! I was really lucky. If I had stayed on that path just a couple of steps more, he'd have got me. To add insult to injury, he then started shooting at me. As it turned out, the village was loaded with bad guys, and a substantial firefight ensued. Before it was over, two of our boys were killed.

Letter to Bill Simmons: dated April 15th, describing this incident:

April 15th

Dear Bill,
I got your letter over a week ago and am just now getting time to answer it. When I received your letter, I was with a tank div. It was just like a WWII movie. A person would climb on top one of these iron horses and ride around all day. We left there and moved up to the DMZ[1], trying to help the Marines. I hate to say it, but the Marines are good.[2] Right now, my Co is awaiting shipment back to our neck of the woods, the Central Highlands—Home of the 1st Cav.

I am going to try to relate the first week spent here at the DMZ, for it was a real hell-raiser. We were flown into here by choppers— This is a Marine Camp called Montezuma—and dug in for the night. The next day we air assaulted out about 20,000 meters to our direct north. From there we began a 6-day march around this point until we were about 10,000 meters south of Montezuma. I have never been so scared as I was in this 6-day period. Charlie never let up on his snipping. It got to a point where we would march way into the night, and then set up, that way we could get a little sleep.

In one three-day period we suffered 10 casualties, 6 in one day. This isn't from pitched battles, but from sniper fire. It got to a point where the zing of a round going past your ear had little effect on your numbed nerves. For example, one day we were to be lifted out of the area. So, we set up a landing zone for the choppers and estab-lished a perimeter. The choppers came in and our men—Second Plt.—ran out and climbed aboard. For some reason the choppers didn't take off, but just sat there. The men climbed off and started milling around, waiting to see what was up. I have never seen choppers set on the ground in an unsecured area before, so I was baffled. I sat down on a rice paddy and started reading a letter that I was just handed.[3]

I was about halfway through when Charlie opened up. In about a 5 to 10 second period he had killed 2 and severely wounded another. Needless to say, my ass was planted in the nearest hole. I couldn't fire my weapon because a squad was in direct line with Charlie and me. There I simply steeled down and continued reading. I am not trying to give you the impression that being fired at doesn't scare the hell out of me, but you get to the point where you just don't give a damn. When it's your time, it's your time.

The day before yesterday is the closest it has come to be my time. Bill, you know I am not a religious man, but by all rights, I should have been messed up. I guess, or should I say I know that the Man was looking after me. We were going to sweep into this reported friendly village. We formed into an assault file and began our approach to the village. To make a shorter story out of it, I will leave out details. We were about 25–50 meters from the village fence when a mine exploded just a matter of feet in front of me. It spun me around and left me in bewilderment. As the smoke started gathering around me, I picked myself up and just in time to hear the crack and zing of a carbine round going over my head. I got to the nearest cover, and a G.I. to my right flank put a stop to the incoming fire. When the smoke cleared my sergeant lay on the ground, and a G.I. was being patched up by the medic. The mine had got both of them, and they were both behind me. We found out later it was self-detonating mine, you know, the kind where a guy stands off in some bushes and waits for someone to walk by, then presses two wires together & boom! By the way you don't say anything about this to Jan, for you are about the only one I tell war stories.

Now for the better side of VN (Vietnam). We have been out in the field since the 7th of March, with no let up. The rumor has it that we will go back to our Base Camp in An Khê for beer, pop, and movies on the 25th of this month. That means clean clothes and a shower.[4] Well I better close for now, write and study.

Tim

Assigned Platoon RTO (Radio Transmitter Operator)

I bring this up now because in the following pages there will be numerous references to the RTO and its role within the Platoon structure. Sometime in mid-April, I was removed from the machine gun crew and reassigned to the position of the Platoon's RTO (Radio Telephone Operator); a position I held for the next eight months. The RTO is selected from the ranks of the company's riflemen. He was still an eleven Bravo, an infantry rifleman, a ground pounder who happened to be assigned the responsibility of carrying the platoon radio and thus carrying out platoon communication. His qualifications: a strong back, rank of an enlisted man, and hopefully the ability to think clearly under stress. Because of the extra weight, about twenty-six pounds, he must at all times carry, the strong back is, no doubt, his greatest attribute.

The advantage of this assignment, besides the prestige that came with it, was that one always knows just about everything happening involving the platoon. Where it was going, and what to expect once it got there. The RTO and the Platoon Leader must at all times remain in close proximity to one another. But not too close, while never too far away. Always around but never giving away the Lieutenant's position by the action of his RTO. The downside of this assignment is two-fold, carrying the extra weight and the damn antenna always waving overhead which clearly identified him to the bad guys.

An unsolicited forewarning often reiterated to an RTO was that an established tactic of the NVA was to, first, identify the RTO (which is easily done by the waving antenna) and take him out, then the first man to his side will probably be the officer in charge. Eliminate him, and you have both cut off communication and killed the leader. All of which makes the Platoon RTO feel really good while walking through the hinterland. I believe that I encountered this during the battle of June 21st. Of course, one always believes that every shot being fired during a firefight is aimed at him.

One of my responsibilities as Platoon RTO was to keep track of, or memorize, what were commonly called "Papa Oscars" or more precisely points of origin." These were nothing more than specific locations on a map, "funny book" in RTO lingo, which were given names. Using these as a reference the RTO could keep the CP (Command Post) informed as to the Platoon's location in relation to an established point of origin or reference any location on a particular map as the need may arise. These reference points and their names were constantly in a state of flux, all of which made it quite confusing. A common communication would go something like this. "Six, three, six, India go. 'Six, India, three, six, India go.' 'Six, India, from Papa Oscar, ranch, uniform three, plus two; Romeo, four plus four. Out." Translated it meant that the Third Platoon RTO has called the Company Commander's RTO and told him that the platoon was located from a specific reference point named Ranch up three and a fourth sections and to the right of this point four and a fourth sections. Confusing I know, but one got very used to such communications.

The Papa Oscars were routinely written down on my trouser legs, names on one leg and locations on the other. Their order in relation to one another was reversed for security reasons, switching names and locations. A few false names and locations were thrown in just to confuse their real identity and location. This practice was well known by my close friend Parks and the Platoon Leader. Each knew that if something happened to me that they could if needed, retrieve my pants and thus retrieve the Papa Oscars. I believe the Platoon Leader also maintained a list of the current Papa Oscars, but do not recall them referring to these. They instead would, for simplicity, rely on me to keep track of all this. The importance of knowing where these points were located on a map together with their assigned name was obviously vital to the security of the Platoon.

I was somewhat blessed with the skill of using a compass, together with reading our funny books to keep track of our exact location. For some reason, I've never been able to figure out why the various platoon leaders I served under did not seem particularly apt at doing this. It just wasn't their strong suit. Therefore, while not in my pay grade, map reading was nevertheless my responsibility, as well as communicating these back to our CP on an ongoing basis. We were generally required to confirm our location every two hours.

To me, the position of Platoon RTO was the best assignment in the platoon. I enjoyed prestige within the unit and was pleased to maintain this position throughout the remainder of my time with the Platoon.

---

1. All references to DMZ were wrong, actually moved to the southernmost part of "I" Core, the Marines operation zone. Many miles away from the DMZ. But that's where we thought we were at the time
2. Bill was a Marine
3. Not so, actually I went back to reading a very sexy book that I had been reading while waiting for the choppers to coming in.
4. The rumor was wrong, we wouldn't see base camp for another month.

FUN TIME IN VACATION LAND

After leaving Montezuma, somewhere around April 17th, we headed for more familiar territory, the Central Highlands and Bồng Sơn Plains, and resumed Company and Platoon sized search and destroy missions. Our mission had us working in a mountainous area, and while there, I came down with a knee infection on my left leg (later thought to be a staph infection that reoccurred several times in later years). In short order, I was running a high fever, and my leg had swollen substantially in size. The Platoon medic Docimo was trying all his magic to keep it under control, but finally, he ordered me back to the MASH Unit at LZ Uplift. After three or four days in a field hospital, the cyst on my knee exploded. I recall calling the doctor over and showing him what had just happened. His response was "Good, that's what we've been waiting for."

He called an aid over, and together they held me down as the doctor squeezed my knee, rendering out the infection. I damn near passed out from the pain, cussing as the medics proceeded with their painful assault on my leg. Finally, it was over, and a speedy recovery ensued. While in Vietnam, I was shot, hit by shrapnel, and had a punji stake go through my leg, but this assault on my knee was the most painful thing that happened to me. Shortly thereafter, I learned that my company was also in LZ Uplift, pulling perimeter security and running day patrols in the nearby hills. Upon learning this I requested to be discharged from the hospital, explaining that I would do nothing more than help with night security from one of our assigned bunkers. They agreed and back to my company I went.

This type of duty was considered a break, or rest, for the company involved. Most of the time was spent sitting around during the day and pulling a shift of guard duty at night. On occasion, a platoon is sent out on patrol, and often a squad goes out on a night ambush. But, in most cases, it is considered good duty.

Upon returning to my platoon, I discovered we had a new Platoon Leader, who replaced Lt. Derr who was shot on Hill 55. The new Lieutenant, Lt. Wagner, was a fairly tall, lanky, good-natured young fellow. We made our introductions, and he informed me that I would be resuming my duty assignment as his RTO, which suited me fine. I liked the guy from the start, and we continued to be very close companions until his death on June 21st.

That night was my first and last encounter with pot. Marijuana was in general use by a number of the boys, and it was not uncommon for them to light up when back in a relatively secure area like LZ English. Somehow, on this evening, they were finally able to convince both Parks and me to try a marijuana cigarette; big mistake. After a few puffs and nothing happening, I was beginning to wonder what all the shouting was about. Then, blackout; all I can remember is lying on top of a bunker with the world spinning overhead. There was also a feeling that I was living in a slow-motion world. I rolled over and began to fall off the top of the bunk. No worries, it seemed as though I had all day to get my feet back under me. I recall being down on the ground, face up looking at the stars with the feeling that my stomach was a volcano with streaks of lightning coming down on me. That was about it, I had survived my first and last encounter with marijuana. As for Parks, he ended up crawling on all fours through the perimeter barbwire. Back home some years later, Parks and I discussed this encounter. Parks being far more informed, or should I say familiar, via in-depth personal knowledge on the subject than I, stated his belief that the boys had set us up by lacing the marijuana with something, thus the strange effect. Yea, those boys got us good. Great laugh for them, bad night for us. The only good to come of it being that I never wanted to go through anything like that again.

The following day it was learned that some of my friends were going on a joy ride out of Uplift intending to catch a ride to an Air Force base called Phù Cát. Here one could get a hot meal, including fresh milk, a hot shower, and all the beer one wanted. So, off we went in the back of a deuce and a half (*military flatbed truck*). Along the way one of the fellows noticed a beer brothel; that in itself was not unusual, but this one had an "OFF LIMITS" sign posted across the front of the building. "Hold it, stop this truck!" Off we got, with instructions to the driver to pick us up on his way back, and in we went. The magnetism of the "sign was too much for us to pass up. After all, we were the Mongoose Bravo; the meanest sons-of-bitches in the valley and no MP was going to tell us where we could or could not go. You know, we believed that. After all, what were the powers that be going to do? Put us in the infantry and send us to Vietnam?

A little side note here: No, we didn't have permission to leave Uplift. It was stupid of us to be alone in the middle of nowhere. Sam may control the day in this area, but Charlie controls the night. Alone, like we were, we were asking for trouble. Our Company officers would not have taken it kindly if they became aware of our little joy ride. Regardless, I did take joy rides like this more than once. Fortunately, nothing ever came of it. It was a dumb thing to do. But whoever said that I was the sharpest pencil in the pack?

The place was quite tame by Vietnam standards, an old Mamasan, together with three younger girls and buckets of cold native beer being the attractions. I guess most of the G.I.s who constantly traveled the adjacent road heeded the "Off Limits" sign, the place was empty except for us. Substantial beer was consumed, with no one paying attention to the girls. Sensing a 'No Sale,' they joined us in what was a fun, extended round of conversation, discussing who knows what, but I do recall enjoying the company. Finally, Mamasan tiring of no takers for her girls walked over to one of them, who was quite attractive by any standard. This girl, probably no more than eighteen or twenty, was fairly tall and from what I could tell possessed an ample figure under her typical black pajama bottoms and light cotton blouse. Wearing no bra, she bounced with each step. Mamasan positioned herself behind the unsuspecting number one girl, then reached over and pulled the girls blouse up over her head. My God, this gal had stateside, *Playboy* boobies, I had never seen the likes of and were totally unknown in Vietnam. The girl squirmed and twisted, but the deed had been done. I recall this young beauty actually blushing as she rearranged her blouse. Mamasan's actions did the trick, the next thing I knew off goes one of my companions into the back room. About this time, our transportation back to Uplift arrived, anxious to get back. We paid up and left our little piece of paradise. To this day, whenever I think of great knockers, this young gal comes to mind. Today, I guess you would have to say she was definitely a ten.

Letter to Bill Simmons:

May Day Hi,
Things are really going well. The last two weeks have been a sham-
mers par adise. (SHAM = gold bicker, cutting, slack, etc...) About 10
days ago or so, we were up in the mountains humping our asses off
when my leg became infected, which turned into a cyst on my knee.

Well, they sent me into a field hospital to lie around. The field
hospital is located at a large LZ (landing zone) called Uplift. After
three days at the hospital, my buns were sore from shots, and I was
bored to death. As luck would have it my company came into the
LZ to pull security on the 3ʳᵈ day. I told the doc that they were in,
so he released me, and I have been lying in this bunker ever since.
Yesterday the Co Medic (Docimo), an RTO (Storie), and I hoped a
ride down the road to the nearest village. Since the area isn't consid-
ered secure, we were fully combat-ready.

You should have seen us as we entered the village whore house, bar combination and laid our M16s & 45s on the bar and asked for some beer. We had a ball there. Being a good married man, I am strictly an observer, not a patron. No kidding. There were two young girls there between ages 16 to 20 or somewhere around there. Age is very hard to tell on these people. Well, getting back to the story. We were sitting there drinking our beer and enjoying things when we heard laughter. Looking around, I saw the Mamasan playing with the bust of the No. 1. girl, well we all burst out in laughter. At that Mamasan pulled the young girls blouse up revealing her unaltered body. It was too much for Storie the RTO. "How Much?" Until this time, we were strictly drinking patrons— 500Ps (Meaning the equivalent of $5.00) was the reply from Mamasan. "Go to hell you bull shit G.I." was Storie's prompt response. He looked over at the young whore. "400P for No. 1 girl" Mamasan nodded her approval and Storie and the young beauty disappeared to the slats.

No sooner had he entered the room when the truck we had prearranged to pick us up pulled in. "Storie, let's go." After a little commotion Storie emerged from the back room, and we climbed into the back of the truck and headed back for the LZ. Well, we were fairly well juiced up on native beer by then, so the Doc (told) the driver to come as close to the natives along the road as he could. As the truck would pass by, the medic would lean over and grab their hats. I never laughed so hard since I've been over here. I think that tomorrow a few of us are going back to town. We couldn't go today because they put us on a damn 15-minute alert. Rumor has it that we are going back to Base Camp sometime soon.

I sure hope so. How is everything back home? Are you improving on your algebra? I do hope so, for I know you can do it if you'll just not let it get you down. Write soon, for I do enjoy hearing from home. It helps break up the day by day routine. When I return to the States I will probably be processed through at Ft Lewis, Washington. If

*you are in Washington I will come by and see you before going on
to Calif.*

Write soon,
Tim

Sometime following the day at the "Off Limits" brothel the
platoon was flown to LZ Hammond. I could be wrong about the
timing of this but believe the third week in April was fairly close.
There is no reference to this in my diary; therefore, I'm guessing
when it occurred. This was actually my second time in Hammond.
The first occurred sometime in early April. We flew in, spent the
night on the runway and flew out early the next morning. All I
remember of that visit was that a hot dinner was provided, and hush
puppies were available for dessert. I also recall that there was a two-
holer adjacent to the runway. Hard to believe that an outhouse is
worthy of comment but then, at the time, being able to sit while
taking a crap was a luxury. I recall Parks and I sitting there for some
time just talking and enjoying the comfort of the two-holer. Go figure,
times were tough and comforts few and far between.

Hammond contained a large Army-controlled runway (in contrast
to belonging to the Air Force) that could accommodate larger fixed-
wing four-engine plains and was located fairly close to Phù Cát Air
Force Base. Highway 1 ran just a mile or so to the west, and there was
a large singular mountain on its northeastern border. Atop this
mountain was a radio relay station. Our mission on this visit was to
provide a portion of base security.

The base was fairly large and contained an artillery battery as
well as both an officer's and an enlisted/NCO club. On this, the
second visit and shortly after getting settled, Lt. Wagner suggested
that he and I get a beer at the officer's club.

"No Wag, you know I can't go in there."

"Bullshit, you're my RTO, and I'm responsible for a section of base
security and must remain in constant radio contact, so let's go"; in we
went. I felt as though I was the boy caught with his fingers in the

cookie jar, all eyes upon me. The unasked question being, "What the hell is this enlisted man doing in here." I had the impression that every officer in the place felt that somehow, I had contaminated it, causing the room to shake, their beer to go green and the paint to peel from the walls. I really wanted out of there. Actually, the place was dead by any standard, so I suggested that we go over to the EM/NCO club where things would definitely be livelier. Like most infantry officers in the field, Lt. Wagner wore no sign of rank, so in we went. No questions asked, and we had a good time.

Unfortunately, later that afternoon things started to unravel, with the EM/NCO club becoming the center of controversy. The club was under the control of the artillery battery previously mentioned. Their rules, they were the boss, and they wanted our boys to leave their weapons outside the club. Now for an infantryman that's an absolute no-no. We're never without our rifles. The only concession we were willing to make is that we would take a round out of the rifle chamber while inside. Not good enough. The counter-offer was, OK, just stack your rifles against the wall adjacent to where we were sitting. Agreed, and so, for a short period all was good. That is, until one of our boys, who was wearing a Colt 45 on his hip, got into a conversation with the bartender, who asked to see the 45. Out it came and presented to the bartender. He fumbles around with it for a few minutes and in the process pulls back the hammer. Un-knowing that the pistol was loaded the bartender proceeds to pull the trigger sending a round through the ceiling. That did it. Out! We had really pissed them off. "Get out and don't come back." We were relieved of our security duty the next day and soon found ourselves back in the real war. This story continued to bring laughter every time it was retold, with a few additions "of course." It amazed me how a story, such as this and the one involving Sin City could change over time to the point where I'm not sure as to what actually happened. Again, I wasn't in the EM/NCO Club at the time of the incident. However, in this case I believe I'm pretty close.

One strange thing did happen while on patrol out of LZ Hammond. We encountered a few bad guys, and a short firefight ensued. This resulted in one of the bad guys getting shot with an M79 grenade round. A 79-grenade is an explosive projectile shot from a shoulder-fired weapon (called an M79). The round itself is about an inch and a half in diameter (40MM) and unfired about 2.5" in length. For it to explode, it must rotate a given number of rotations after being fired. This, of course, is to protect the shooter from blowing himself up because of him being too close to the impact area.

The gook got hit in the chest, where it did penetrate but did not explode. The reason being that it probably didn't get enough rotations to arm itself. Regardless, there he lay with the bulging unexploded 79 round in his chest. Of course, no one wanted to get near him. We didn't know if the round would explode or not. Eventually, we reached the conclusion it was probably safe to evacuate the poor fellow back to a MASH unit. But still, we weren't sure. Later it was learned the doctor responsible for removing the round was also very hesitant to operate for fear of it exploding. Can you imagine the look on the face of that poor doctor when first seeing this bulging grenade? I guess he finally did remove it. But still, what would you do?

The company did have an opportunity to return to LZ Hammond some months later to provide security while the base was deactivated. During our short stay, we would see the last big four-engine plane land and take off from Hammond. Yes, the last plane did receive incoming fire as it sat on the runway. While waiting around for orders for us to take our leave and with little to do, the guys started to gather and socialize. Nothing good ever occurs when a G.I. has too much time on his hands. Poor decisions will usually be made, but I can assure you that they will be humorous. My close and still good friend Buzzy Suman decided he was going to take a shot at a horse some two to three hundred yards away and on the other side of the base wire perimeter.

"No Buzz, you don't mean it, you can't do that."

"Yea Mac, I'm going to see if I can hit that horse from this distance."

"No Buzzy you really don't mean that." Well, he didn't shoot the horse, and to this day I don't know if he really meant it or was just pulling my leg. I don't know, but the horse didn't get shot. However, that's not the real story arising from our last stay at Hammond.

While waiting for the last of the last big planes to leave the base an unprovoked murder of a Vietnamese civilian took place. It was concluded that someone with Mongoose Bravo purposely shot and killed a young civilian. Apparently, the victim was waiting at the wire perimeter for the base's final closure. Once closed, he and a number of other civilians that had gathered would then breach the wire perimeter in order to glean the area of any valuable left-behinds.

Lt. Barret, (this happening taking place after June 21st and the death of Lt. Wagner. Barret or Big Skinny as we referred to him was the new platoon leader), and I were some distance from where the shooting took place when we first got wind of it. The story conveyed at the time was that a young man was caught trying to climb through the perimeter wire and was shot. If so, that would make it a legal shooting. I'm not trying to excuse what took place, but let's not forget we had earlier received incoming rounds as the last plane landed and took off, as well as receiving occasional incoming throughout the day. So, we were on edge not knowing what to expect.

On receiving word of the shooting, Lt. Barret dispatched a squad to the hillside overlooking where the shooting took place, and he and I went to investigate. A fairly large number of civilians had gathered and were creating quite a fuss, and we would be standing out in the open amongst the hostile crowd. I conveyed to Big Skinny that I was concerned about our standing out in the open like this. We had no defense in case hostile action did break out. The Lt. pulled out his 45, and I laid my M16 across my arms with the safety off as we approached. The fire team previously placed about fifty yards uphill from where the body lay, provided us with some degree of security. When we got where the body was laying, it was on our side of the wire.

The crowd of civilians that had gathered were, except for the parents of the slain civilian, on the other side. They indicated that the slain civilian was on his side of the wire when shot and that a G.I. had in fact gathered up the body and pulled it into the base. This was later believed to be the truth. Big Skinny ordered the gathered crowd to disperse, or he would order his men to fire upon them. With wisdom, the better form of valor, the group thinned out except for the immediate family of the slain man. By this time, they had climbed through the wire and were standing over the body of their son. They were right in our face giving us holy hell. They kept pointing at the members of the fire team indicating that one of them did the shooting. They kept pointing their finger at Docimo, our medic who fit their description of the shooter. The South Vietnamese police were immediately informed of the incident, and in short order a contingent of them arrived and took command of the area and incident.

The investigation into this shooting lingered for what seemed months without resolution. Poor Docimo was put through the ringer but continued to proclaim his innocence. An informant was placed in our platoon, but he failed to learn anything. There was absolutely no discussion among the boys of the platoon on the subject of who shot the civilian. It was as though the incident never happened. All was quiet, and I continued to suspect poor Docimo.

After months of investigation, the matter was finally closed with no conclusion as to who officially shot the guy. All I knew was I had my suspicions that were totally wrong, and I didn't learn the shooter's identity for some months. It wasn't until arriving home that Parks finally filled me in as to what took place. I had been left uninformed and out of the loop by the rest of the guys. I would assume, due to my position and closeness with Lt. Barret, and correctly assuming that if known I would have informed the powers that be. "So, don't tell Mac, he'll tell Big Skinny." So much for the one murder I knew of while in Vietnam. A totally unnecessary death; among so many unnecessary deaths.

A total screw up, and yes, they were right, I would have told. The actual shooter was one of our senior NCOs.

BACK TO AN KHÊ, AND CIVILIZATION

*May 17th Went into English to An Khê right out to Camp Action,
Artillery.*
May 18th Stayed at Camp Action. Mad minute at 12 and 2:00.
*May 19th Went down to bridge & swam. I bought beer from a little
girl.*
*May 22nd Went to An Khê for a couple of hours and tried to get
mustache on I.D.*
Jun 1st Out to the XYZ Ring.

From March 8th, 1967, the day following the Mongoose being
kicked out of An Khê because of the little misunderstanding in
Sin City until May 17th the Company was, except for the occasional
pulling of security guard at one of the foreword LZs, continually in
the jungle, villages, and mountains, away from any sort of civilization
and continually resupplied by air. Unfortunately, a number of those
who departed on the 8th of March would not hear the band play or
share in any of the donuts handed out by the donut-dollies, cele-

brating our return to our home base in An Khê two and a half months later.

We remained in the An Khê area for a month (May 17 – Jun 19). The duty was good, with our being immediately trucked to Camp Action and bridge security. Four or five days later we were at Mustang and from there, patrolling and pulling night ambushes in An Khê's, XYZ zone. Mustang is actually just a barrack and helicopter landing pad within the secured area of our Base Camp at An Khê. Its function is to provide a ready action force made up of an infantry platoon that can be dropped into a battle on a moment's notice. Fortunately, all we did while there was watch movies (*that's where I saw "To Sir With Love"*) and play football. Thank God all was quiet on the western front during our stay. From Mustang we flew out to the XYZ zone which is an imaginary set of bands or rings surrounding An Khê, denoting defensive positions. We were actually four or five miles out from Base Camp. I recall the jungle could be quite thick in this area when, for some unknown reason, it would open into small grassland areas.

While at Camp Action, which was an artillery firebase located on Highway 163/19 approximately four or five miles east of An Khê, we had a chance to go swimming in one of the small creeks. It was here that I first met Mie, a little 14-year-old Vietnamese girl. She and a couple of other little girls had ridden their bikes out to where we were and sold us some native Coca-Cola. Yes, they really did bottle Coke in Vietnam.

I would run across this little girl numerous times after this, and we became very good friends. There are numerous stories I could tell about her, Parks, her family, and our friendship. Whenever in the An Khê area, I would see Mie. It was not unusual for me to spend the better part of a day with her and her family while Parks and other members of the unit went off to Sin City. Parks and I enjoyed kidding Mie that we were taking her with us when we returned to the States.

Her response was always the same, "Oh no, I can't leave my father or brother." However, on this one occasion, just before my return home, she said: "Yes, take me with you to America."

I responded, telling her, "You know Mie, we can't do that."

"I know Sergeant Mac, I know."

Somewhere about this same time, I asked her what she would do if the war didn't turn out the way we wanted. As I think back on her response, it pretty well sums up the reality of the Vietnam War. "Sergeant Mac, don't worry, don't you know me VC too." It is enough to say that a couple of days prior to my departure from Vietnam, I was with her and family, and her telling me with tears in her eyes, "Sergeant Mac, I love you same, same as my brother." This little girl has stayed with me, in my thoughts my entire life. Did she survive? Did she pull it off and convince the lords of her land that she too is VC?

I hoped so. She was my one and only true Vietnamese friend. I told you that I was hardened—*yea, sure*. This little girl really meant a lot to me.

Jan and I, together with my daughter and granddaughter Kiley, returned to Vietnam in April 2017, and I was able to relocate Mie and have dinner with her. She lived a hard life, losing a child to the war, but she did survive.

THE MAJOR BATTLE OF JUNE 21, 1967

Jun 17th Birthday. Spent on XYZ Range. Played cards.
Jun 18th Getting ready to move out.
Jun 19th Moved to Uplift. 2/5th made contact, we're held on call.
June 20th On call at Uplift for 2/5th hit hard, just over the hill.
June 21st Got wounded at Van Thien 3 medevac to Uplift from Quan Nhon.
Jun 25th Transferred to Cam Rhan Bay hospital.
Jul 18th Left Cam Rhan for Field (Base Camp, An Khê)

I spent my 26th birthday out on the XYZ ring, a rainy day, cold night, and a world away from home, family, and friends. On the afternoon of June 19^{th,} the Mongoose was airlifted out of An Khê to LZ Uplift. We were leaving the relative comfort of the last month and going back to the shooting gallery, the real world of Vietnam. The Company had been reinforced with a fairly large number of replacements, with the Third Platoon receiving four or five of them. Therefore, the strength of the Platoon was high, numbering in the high twenties. Two of these newbies were to become good friends, Houser and Curtis. Both of which will be knitted into the fabric of this writing later on. Curtis has gone ahead and written his own accounting of these times, incorporating them into a novel. Curtis and I have remained in contact to this day. Unfortunately, I lost track of Houser. I know he survived and was from Kent, Washington.

A sister company from the 2/5th had come under heavy contact on the coast, not far from our current location. The Mongoose was placed in reserve to come to their aid if needed. The next 2 ½ days were spent on the runway at Uplift, waiting to join them in battle. I remember that both days were exceptionally hot, with us just stuck there, hurry—waiting, hurry—waiting, no shade, sitting and sleeping in the dirt next to the runway, with no way to escape the incessant heat, nowhere to go, just waiting to be inserted into the melee alongside our sister company. It never came to be.

Fairly early during the morning of June 21st, while still sitting on the runway at Uplift, we got word of a suspected NVA hospital, located somewhere in the hills on the Phu My side of the Phu My/Phu Cat boundary, near the village complex of Van Thien. The Mongoose was to go and check it out. That was all the information shared with the boys carrying the rifles. This type of mission was not unusual, such intelligence often came down to us and was almost always wrong. We inadvertently believed that like so many other false reports, this one would amount to nothing. Therefore, we were not especially vigilant, or concerned, as we moved out for the day's trek through Neverland. It was just another glorious day in Vietnam. This lack of concern was our first, but certainly not our last, mistake of the day. Had we known what we were about to walk into—our don't give a damn arrogance would have transmuted to one of trepidation. This could have or should have been resolved by merely sharing with the grunts the intelligence concerning this operation. A stupid mistake often made by those in charge. Would the sharing of this information have actually changed anything—I don't know? Probably not. But I do believe we would have been better mentally prepared for what was to transpire before the day was out.

Shortly after a hot breakfast at Uplift, choppers airlifted us to an area located about 500 yards south and to the east of a village named Van Thien 3 (*see map in endnote*). Evidently incoming rounds were fired at some of the helicopters during our landing; which should have put us on extreme alert, but for some unknown reason, it didn't. (2nd *mistake of the day*) The only excuse for me personally being the chopper I was in was not targeted. The actual landing and securing of the area, other than the chatter on the radio about the incoming rounds, was uneventful.

With all of B Company on the ground and the area secured, the Company Commander dispatched the 1st Platoon into the hills to the northeast, looking for the suspected hospital. I had no idea at the time that a captured NVA soldier would be leading the 1st Platoon to the enemy hospital. My platoon, the 3rd, took up a defensive position to the south of where the Company Commander had set up his Command Post (CP). As luck would have it, this just so happened to be the Company Commander's first day of commanding a combat infantry company in a hostile area. I am sure that it is a day he will never forget.

I recall watching the 1st Platoon for some time as its men worked their way up into the mountains in search of the supposed hospital, while we, the 3rd Platoon, remained in our defensive position. We were pretty laid back, half-stepping (*not paying attention*), not really expecting much to happen. We anticipated a day that would be taken up by sitting on our asses, waiting on the 1st Platoon's presumed empty-handed return. It didn't take long for four of us; Lieutenant Wag (Wagner), Assistant Gunner Parks, myself and someone else (*I don't remember who*), to find a comfortable spot and to get a card game going. The Lieutenant had spent the better part of a month trying to teach us the fundamentals of playing Bridge. Our attention was devoted to this undertaking for about 15 to 30 minutes, all was going well—the world was good.

Word came in over the radio that an observation chopper spotted what he thought was suspicious activity in the form of an NVA soldier in the village of Van Thien 3 located some three hundred yards of open rice paddy to the west of the CP, where the

Company Commander would be located. For some reason, I've never understood why, the Old Man (*Company Commander*) dispatched a seven-man squad, consisting of four members of the Weapon Platoon, to go and investigate the reported sighting. While members of a weapons platoon are technically classified as infantry-men, they do not have the same training, nor do they carry out day to day activities of an infantry rifleman. They, in short, should not have been assigned this task. Their job is to fire the mortar and other such close support weapons. Some of the men making up this detail included our top-ranking NCOs: 1ˢᵗ Sgt. (*Top Sgt. Dennison*), Weapon Platoon's Plt. Sgt. SSG Morris, Sgt. Tom Johnson, a good friend by the name of Zachery and our former Platoon Sergeant, Sgt. Vieth.

Why the Old Man didn't send us, a straight leg well-seasoned light infantry platoon is baffling. The Third Platoon, with the exception of Lt. Wagner, who had been in-country only a couple of months and those previously mentioned 4 or 5 newbies who joined the Platoon in June, was made up of experienced, battle-hardened rifle-men; survivors of many shoot-um-up encounters with the North Viet-namese Army. Not that we wouldn't have received the same reception suffered by the weapon platoon, but our chances of survival would have been much better, and the company would not have lost the service of three of its senior NCOs and its Mortar Platoon. (*Mistake number 4*).

Within what now seemed only a few minutes, we heard a lot of shooting, followed by word again on the radio that a number of those unfortunate members of the ill-conceived weapon squad were down, either wounded, killed or just hugging dirt, in an open rice field on the outskirts of Van Thien 3. At the time, we had no idea as to who was alive or dead but later learned three were killed during the initial burst of gunfire and three wounded, and a fourth was unhurt. The wounded included the Company 1ˢᵗ Sgt. Denison, our old Platoon Sgt. Vieth and SPC 4 Ronny Zachary. The one that was not hurt hugged mother earth and played dead until he could be extracted. My friend, SSG Morris, the weapons platoon sergeant who had encouraged me following my first firefight and who had only a week or so to go before going home, was among those killed.

Now, with people dead and dying in an open rice field, the 3ʳᵈ Platoon was finally given the green light to move out and position itself for an extraction of what was left of the weapon squad. In short, the 3ʳᵈ Platoon was to cross the same open ground that proved to be the killing field for the weapons squad, get itself into the village and engage the enemy and suppress enemy fire. A good day was quickly turning to shit. Thus, went the morning of that fateful day, the 21ˢᵗ of June, the summer solstice and thus the longest day of the year in 1967.

Before this day was over a lot of good young men, from both opposing armies, who would have rather been somewhere else, would find themselves drawn into a series of events not of their making, that would test their will, go a long way in shaping their future character, and for far too many be the last day of their lives. Sons, brothers, husbands, and fathers; each with another life to live in another place, from varying social backgrounds; two opposing armies from separate continents were by some strange twist of fate about to clash in a struggle for survival. Who were these sons, brothers, and fathers of the 1ˢᵗ Cav? And who were these poor simple sons-of-bitches conscripted into the 7ᵗʰ battalion, of the 18ᵗʰ Regiment of the North Vietnamese Army? And, most troubling, who were those uncountable villagers; innocent men, women, and children; who would, due to no fault of their making, perish that day. What would their lives have been if fate had not placed them in that far away village on this particular day. The carnage inflicted on those innocent villagers is something I cannot shake. It continues to weigh on me to this day. However, at the time the destruction of the village by artillery and air power was viewed as a necessary trade-off to save numerous G.I.s lives.

Lt. Wagner called upon two of his squads to form the initial assault force, while the third, together with one of the Platoon's two M60 machine guns, moving to our right flank, held their position and provided covering fire. The assaulting two squads, numbering 14 or 15 seasoned riflemen, would be working in tandem with Lt. Wagner, one of the two M60 machine guns, and myself. We would attempt to cross the open rice field from its south and secure a front inside the village. The idea was to get our troops between those down and dying in the open rice paddy and the North Vietnamese direct line of fire. With that accomplished a successful evacuation of our fallen brothers could be undertaken. To accomplish this, we had to cross some three or four hundred yards of the open, dry rice paddy and fight our way into the enemy-held village. Now think about it. Less than twenty of us were about to assault a village held by a company of well-seasoned members of the North Vietnamese Army. REALLY! Who thought this one up? I'm being too hard here. No one knew at the beginning of our assault what was in that Village. However not long after the assault began, we did receive word that we were up against a heavy weapons, reinforced company; which amounted to a defending force of over one hundred. I believe, but could be wrong, that we made this initial assault without either air or artillery support. The reason for this would have been due to the downed ill-fated weapon squad and their close proximity to the village.

What was left of the weapons squad lay to our left flank, about 50 yards northeast of our proposed line of attack and about twenty to thirty yards from the village. As indicated, one of our two platoon's M60 machine guns would accompany our assault; the other, manned by friends, Parks and Little and a new kid by the name of Ronald Houser, would move off to our right flank with the remaining 3rd Squad and hopefully force the enemy to keep their heads down while we crossed the field. The two squads making the initial advance on the village would alternate between assaulting, then holding position and providing supporting fire as the alternate squad moved forward in its assault. Lt. Wagner and I would work our way between the two squads. In this manner the rice field was successfully crossed, moving about 20 to 30 yards with each alternating advance. In all, it probably took no more than 30 to 45 minutes to make the crossing, during which the shooting was intense. The noise thus created would forever be imprinted in my mind. Remarkably, all made it safely across except a forward artillery observer and myself.

If we actually crossed that field in that 30 minutes, it had to be the longest 30 minutes of my life. Most of the time was spent in short spurts of advance running, followed by a crawl. Up, run, down, reload and shoot, crawl and then up again, shooting all the time. There was absolutely no cover, except an occasional earthen dike, followed by another 30 yards of open dry paddy. These all too few irrigation check borders were no more than 6 to 8 inches in height. Not much cover for a 200 lb. six-footer to hide behind. I recall that the hot barrel of my M16 had caused several burns on my left forearm. To this day, I carry the scars from laying the hot M16 barrel across my forearm while firing over the top of the shallow irrigation checks. Lt. Wagner either didn't recognize the danger of our position or else he was somehow able to put it out of his mind. This was the first time he was involved in a major firefight, and I don't believe he ever really realized the extent of the danger we were in. He was constantly on the move, crawling, running, always moving from one position to the next, with me stumbling along, not wanting to identify him to the enemy by my close proximity. He continued moving his men in a methodical, steady assault

It was, as previously said, the RTO's duty to stay in the area of his Lieutenant, but never too close as to give up his position. The weight of the 50 plus pounds on my back was wearing me down. Realizing that I couldn't keep up with Lt. Wagner by crawling, I had no alternative but to stand and run from position to position as the Lieutenant crawled across the front of the assault line. The Old Man (*Company Commander*) was constantly on the radio, asking questions. I guess that was his job, but his requests constantly caused me to stand up and run the few steps separating the Lt. from myself, thus exposing myself and the Lieutenant to enemy fire. By standing I believe the enemy was able to figure out where the radio was located. But really what could one say to the CO (*Company Commander*), "yes, we were still trying to cross that damn rice paddy, no the Platoon Leader was not right at hand. No, I wouldn't recommend that I expose him by running up next to him and handing him the radio handset." To me, it made no sense at all for me to unnecessarily expose Lt. Wagner.

Most of the questions I was able to answer, but eventually, he got tired of hearing from me and wanted to talk directly to Lt. Wagner. This resulted in me jumping up and running over to the Lieutenant, so he could tell the Old Man that we are still in the rice field, still advancing. Looking back on it what a silly reason to risk one's life. Where in the hell did he think we were? If he'd got off his dead ass and move his Command Post to the edge of the open rice field, he could see for himself what was going on. Oh, but who am I to question the wisdom of an Army Captain, the Company Commander (on his first day in the field) who had already given up his first line of defense, the Mortar Platoon. (Am I still bitter over the loss of the ill-fated Mortar Platoon, YES, the loss of those men may have been avoidable.) It was during one of the open runs, about 30 yards out from the village, that my luck ran out, and I was hit by what I believe to be a ricochet and fractured SKS rifle round. I remember thinking, *God Damn It Lieutenant, just slow down and find somewhere to take cover.*

Unfortunately, the Lieutenant continued exposing himself to enemy fire until later that day, when he and a 7.62 rifle round came together, with him the worst for the encounter, leaving him with a bullet through the center of his chest. Even then he didn't die until about half an hour later. He was one hell of a man, one of America's best, and a very, very good friend. I think about him often and what a good friend he was. If anyone was a true hero of that battle, it was Lt. Wagner. He was handed an impossible task and got it done, and in the process, single-handed took out two enemy dug in positions that were raining hell on the rest of us. In all the accounts of this day that I have read, none of them recognizes the cool-headed leadership exhibited by Lt. Wagner. He embodied leadership and remains the bravest man I have ever known. Not bad for a momma's boy, which Lt. Wagner was.

The first of our fire teams had already reached the cover of the outskirts of the village when I got shot in the neck. I remember the force of the bullet spinning me backwards. Strangely, it didn't hurt. I reached up, found blood, stumbled to the edge of the village, falling against its raised earthen bank and then putting on a field dressing

(*Bandage*). The bleeding was almost immediately stopped. I would live to fight in a number of yet to come battles.

There are a lot of critters in Vietnam who are out to make life miserable, not the least of these being ants. In fact, to my way of thinking, ants far outpaced the VC (*Viet Cong*) as the number one GOTCH YA. They were relentless, and I landed right in the middle of a bunch of them. We were receiving fire from both flanks, leaving me pretty well pinned down. Nowhere to go, no alternative but to share the real estate on which I sat with these little man-eating critters. Thus, is my vivid memory of being wounded. Hot, thirsty, hurting, and being eaten alive by ants.

The village was elevated about two and a half feet above the floor of the adjacent fields, forming an island of coconut palm, low hedges and thatched roofs, surrounded by open rice paddies. In some strange way, the village itself was quite serene, even charming. Looking down on the village, it was in the shape of an inverted L. We were able to position ourselves in the southeast corner of it, in the center of the L shaped area, with Lieutenant and myself along with the other wounded in middle and our boys taking up positions inside the southern edge of it.

This gave us a secure line forming a V about 50 yards in length. Some members of the Platoon, under the leadership of the Platoon Sergeant who we called Short Round, were able to breach the outer defenses of the village, which resulted in a short-lived, close range, fierce firefight. I believe our boys took out 3 or 4 during this initial assault. Eventually, they were able to secure a frontal position within the village itself. The Platoon Sergeant was killed during this action. One other soldier (*Jinkins*) was seriously wounded while inside the village.

There may have been others wounded or killed; I just don't recall. Now, this is really weird, the Platoon Sgt. was killed while standing up to take a leak. Me, I'd have peed in my pants. Jinkins was able to make it out under his own power and was eventually sent home due to his wounds. The interesting thing about him is he had previously served in the Army and had been discharged. Upon his return home, he took his brother's place, assuming his brother's name in the draft and as such again found himself back in the Army, under the false name of his brother. *(I bet this really gave the VA fits trying to sort out how to award benefits.)*

I sat in my little protected part of the world formed by the village rising from the field, its hedgerows and open rice field to my rear. The radio was relinquished to a former RTO. I assumed the position of chief M16 repairman, unjamming rifles, distributing M16 ammo, and collecting and rationing out available grenades and M79 rounds. One haunting legacy that I have carried with me over the years is the feeling that if I would not have been wounded, and were able to perform my duties of RTO, including keeping my friend, the young Lieutenant in tow, he may have survived that day. Instead, he just kept running around directing action and once too often tempting fate by exposing himself to enemy fire.

As for myself, I was pinned down by the enemy who were located to both my right and left flank. They were firing from dug in positions on the edge of the raised village. From there they could employ automatic fire, keeping myself and another wounded soldier pinned in place. Fortunately, they couldn't get a good angle on us, constantly missing by no more than a couple of feet. I was beat-up, but not bad enough to get a free ride back to the States. The NVA to my left had bad intentions but couldn't quite get a clear shot at me without exposing himself. I recall stretching out my leg, just a little, and having him open up, *rat-a-tat-at-at*. I would pull my leg back just in time. This little scenario was played out several times, with me always pulling my leg back. But, to be honest, I was giving serious consideration to just leaving it out there and saying goodbye to Vietnam and all this over-glorified, ungodly assault on humanity.

Lieutenant Wagner, who until this point had maintained a position next to me, spotted the enemy dug in to our east, or my left. He then crept along the village edge, taking advantage of the hedgerows and recess of the rice field. When adjacent to, and four feet away from the enemy position, he jumped up and started firing, knowing damn well that the enemy soldier would duck back into his hole. The poor

NVA soldier did just as suspected, giving the Lieutenant the opportunity, he was looking for. With the poor bastard ducking down in his hole, not looking up to see what was about to happen, Lt. Wagner simply rolled in a grenade, killing the NVA soldier instantly. We recovered what was left of his SKS rifle and, of all things, his hammock, which I carried throughout the remainder of my tour, putting it often to good use.

This same sneak, shoot, and toss tactic was again tried by the Lieutenant on the NVA soldier located to our right, or east. This was the same one shooting at me. Much to the Lieutenant's surprise, the outcome was much different. Again, the Lieutenant crept along the lower rice field floor, taking advantage of the raised village and hedgerow. Again, getting within a few feet of the enemy position the Lieutenant jumped up while firing his M16, followed by the dropping of the grenade; but this time the enemy didn't just sit there waiting to meet his demise. He instead reached down, picked up the live grenade and threw it back at the totally surprised Lieutenant Wagner. I still remember with a smile, the Lieutenant running across the short section of rice field which separated us, his knees almost reaching his chest as he ran; shouting, "The son-of-a-bitch threw it back, he threw it back." The grenade landed offline and exploded doing no harm. But, that picture of my good friend running across that field, his long and lanky body stretched out in full flight, and his shouting as he ran is one of the more humorous, bittersweet pictures I carry from that war. Following this, the Lieutenant snuck back, except this time he just lobbed a grenade next the enemy position and waited. The NVA soldier, seeing this, simply ducked down into his hole, waiting for the grenade to explode, doing him no harm. The Lieutenant was banking on the NVA soldier doing exactly that, and immediately following the explosion of the grenade, up jumps the Lieutenant, shooting directly down into the poor NVA soldier's hole, killing him in place. Two For The Lieutenant.

We were pinned down in and on the outskirts of the village for what must have been 2 to 3 hours, but help was on the way in the form of two 40 MM track guns (*dusters*), and I believe a single tank.

I'm fuzzy about the tank, but I think one was involved. Immediately upon their arrival, they engaged the enemy and eventually broke the siege. By positioning themselves about 40 to 50 yards out in the open rice field, they were able to fire point-blank into the enemy positions. We took advantage of this to extract the remainder of the Mortar Platoon's dead and wounded, as well as the wounded forward observer, Jinkins, and myself. I recall the Lt. Wag asking, "Mac, are you sure you're ok to make your way back to the CP on your own. Can you run?"

"Yea, I'm ok Wag" Thinking back on it, it was the last words spoken to Lt. Wag. and seeing my close friend alive.

I recall making my way back across the rice field and eventually linking up with the Command Post. There were several other wounded men gathered waiting for extraction. I believe that Doc McWethy the medic from the 1st Platoon may have been there, but I may be wrong. Someone redressed my wound and put me in line for extraction. The Company Commander's RTOs were busy trying to set up a Medevac. Medevac Choppers were in the air but had refused to land. Our savior, also from the sky, was in the form of the workhorse of the 1st Cav., the Slicks (*supply and assault choppers*), whose pilots never let us down, they brought in ammo, water, and other much-needed resupply. These were the same guys who day in and day out brought in our evening meals and whatever else was needed to keep us going. The same guys who flew us in earlier that day.

The next thing I see is here comes the Slicks, regardless of the shooting going on around them, dropping resupply and picking up the dead and dying. Down they came, followed by another and then another and so on until all the wounded were extracted and the Company resupplied.

This is the last of my direct knowledge of the happenings of that day. My understanding of what took place following my extraction is from nightly, foxhole discussions with those, including Parks, Little, Curtis, The Douche, Everhart, the new kid Houser and so many more who were there from start to finish. Before it was all over two members of the Company would be awarded (postmortem) the

Medal of Honor, one of them being Doc McWethy, a conscientious objector, who never carried a rifle while with the Company. I spent the next 27 days in the hospital, with most it being spent in the Cam Ranh Bay recovery center.

I just thought of this: something that took place at the receiving hospital in Quin Nhon. This is the place where you are sent to have whatever surgery you may need. I was what you may call a walking wounded. Not that bad off. I was not going to bleed out or die from my gunshot wound; therefore, following a short chopper ride from LZ Uplift to Quin Nhon I was put in a holding area waiting the receiving nurse's inspection.

I had not seen a round-eyed girl for some time, and she was beautiful. I can picture her to this day. Medium height, dark, short cut hair and large brown eyes—just a beautiful girl of Romanian ancestry. *(How do I know, I asked)* Finally, she calls me forward and directs me to a screened-off area. There she makes some nice introductory remarks, "My name is Lt. ? and I am here to examine you for wounds and get you to a doctor. What's your name? how are you doing? etc., Now I must have you remove your clothes."

"What!"

"Yes, drop your pants."

Remember I haven't seen an American, USA No. 1 prime girl in months and this one wants me to drop my pants. I'm usually not shy in conforming to a medical induced request, but this was different. She noticed my hesitation, and with the biggest smile said, "Look G.I., I do this day in, and day out, there are no surprises." AND WITH THE BIGGEST GRIN EVER SAID, "I KNOW YOU DO NOT HAVE UNDERWEAR ON, NONE OF YOU INFANTRY GUYS EVER DO." Off went my pants leaving me butt naked. It would have been easier if she had been big, fat, and over fifty, but she wasn't. We just carried on with normal, polite conversation as if nothing unusual was going on. Maybe for her there wasn't, but for me it was damn unusual. She informed me as to where she was from, where she went to school, how long she had been in the service and asked me the same. It was just so strange, and she was so beautiful. It all kinda reminded me just what we were fighting for. For all those wonderful USA, home-town girls. Sorry Jan, but she was just so nice and so beautiful. Next thing, in comes two surgeons and after a little probing on to a gurney I go, headed to the operating room, with this beautiful nurse, Lt. Whatever tagging along.

Letters Sent Home Expressing Emotions About the Battle of June 21st

Letter to Bill Simmons:

June 26, 1967

Hi Bill,
I wrote four pages of a letter to you yesterday, and this morning decided to scrap the whole thing. It would have taken another forty pages to even suggest what was in my mind, although I doubt that even then, things would have been left unexplained.

I'm now in a convalescent hospital located at Cam Ranh Bay. It is really something; hot and cold running water, showers, stateside toilets (the kind that flush) and regular mess facilities. I got here yesterday afternoon after being transferred from the hospital at Quin Noun. You wouldn't believe it, the 21st I was flown to Quin Noun, along with 6 other guys from my outfit, for emergency (medical treatment) and on the 25th I am laying on a beach listening to a USO show. That is Army expediency.

I am not going into all the details of the battle in which I got shot, for that is what I tried to do in my other letter. It is too mixed up. I would try and explain one thing and end up having to backtrack to try and give proper background. Maybe in a month or so when I have heard enough accounts of it and have been able to collect the facts and rearrange them into somewhat of a pattern; I'll be able to

*tell you a real good war story. But the way it stands now it is the
most tragic thing I have ever been a part of. From all I can gather
the total stands as this—U.S. 26 WIAs & 11 KIAs—NVA 147 KIAs
by body count and we're still counting when last I heard. The
figures are miss leading, most of our casualties were from my Plt.
(not so, the causalities were pretty evenly scattered, with many
occurring after my departure, and coming from the 1st Plt) We got
torn up. There I go again drifting into a war story. Bill Just you
make sure you keep your bad back (Bill was let out of the Marines
some years earlier with a bad back) This is the only time I have
ever suffered any thought that I might not make it home. From all I
can collect in my mind I should have been sapped a score of times—
just how long can a man's luck hold out.*

*The rest of my outfit, or what's left of it is still out there trying to
pick up the pieces of what there is to gather up. Those poor guys. At
least I am out of it for a while.*

*How is everything at home? What are you doing, and what are
your plans? I guess that it is swimming weather back home—I
think about the river and fast water, Oley (favorite beer of the day)
and rubber raft often. Write when you get a chance.*

Take care,
Tim

July 12, 1967

Hi Simmons Family (Bill),
*Greetings from the sin capital of South East Asia. It looks as if they
are finally catching up with me. I should be kicked out of this place
(Cam Ranh Rehab Hospital) in a couple of days and sent back to
the gallery. DAMN!*

You would not believe this place. The guards run around with empty 45s. Their rifles and other weapons are locked up in some arms room, and they all have spit-shined boots and starched fatigues. (This in comparison to how we lived: locked and loaded always. Our rifles never out of reach. Dirt and grime, we always looked like hell.) *All the patients run around in blue P. Js. and combat boots.*

The head surgeon here goes by the name of The Butcher. A real quack. You should see his work. This one Marine got shot in the arm and had a patch of hide about 3"s blown off. The Butcher skin graphed a patch from his leg. Now the kid has 2 hideous scars and can't use either his arm or leg. Another friend from my company had a hole blown in his back about 4" long and 2" wide. Not very deep ½" or so. The Butcher decided to sew him up—what a mess. A 2-year-old first attempt of quilt work looks better.

July 18th Same Letter:

I am now at the Airport at An Khê headed back to the field. A good thing too, for I have been on a three-day drunk and am now flat broke. There is a strong rumor we're headed to the Cambodian border to help the 173rd. I sure hope not.

I got your letter about the union and their scandal sheet. What a mess, any halfwit should be able to see through them. (I have no idea what this was about—lost in time.)

Well, I had better try and get a letter off to Jan before my plane comes.

Take care,
Tim

FIRE FIGHT OF JULY 25, 1967

Jul 21st Returned to field after recovering from wounds sustained on June 21st.
Jul 22nd Killed VC on patrol outside of Ollie.
Jul 25th Firefight just outside of LZ Uplift. Fought 7th of the 18th. Carried wounded all night. VERY TIRED.
Jul 26th Spent the day on mountain top. Extracted for Uplift.
Jul 27th Left Uplift. Go through villages.

Circumstances found me returning to the Platoon one month to the day following being wounded on June 21st. They were providing security at LZ Ollie. A new Platoon Leader, by the name of Lieutenant Barret, (immediately assigned the nickname of Big Skinny) had joined the Platoon during my absences and following the death of Lt. Wagner on the 21st. Following what amounted to polite introductory conversation, he quickly moved to what was really on his mind. Did I wish to remain as the Platoon RTO or be reassigned to the Old Man (Company Commander) as his RTO.

Evidently, this assignment was going to be made that day. If I wanted to stay with the Platoon and not the Co CP (Command Structure), then I should disappear. I really had no idea as to why the Old Man wanted me as his RTO, but regardless my preference was to stay with the Platoon and therefore chose to vanish for the day. Following my disappearance, I was reassigned 3rd Platoon RTO.

The next day a small group, of perhaps 10 of us, were on patrol, walking no more than a couple of miles out from LZ Ollie when we ran across what we believed to be two VC (Viet Cong) carrying a long pole and heading up into the Tiger Mountains. Most likely the pole was for the construction of a bunker. Or, that's what we believe, so we engaged them, killing one and wounding, but lost the other. It was obvious from the carrying on at the adjacent village that these were two of theirs. I guess that my stay in the hospital had softened me, for I truly felt sorry for the families of these two men. This was for me a most unusual reaction, which I couldn't at the time explain. I had felt bad before seeing children hurt, and the killing of dogs and livestock, but Viet Cong—never.

I've given this some thought over the years. It really troubles me. These two VCSs (Viet Cong suspects) were unarmed and wore no military uniform. Their misfortune was that we were informed that an NVA Unit was suspected to be in the hills which appeared to be the destination of the two. This coupled with the carrying of a pole up into the adjacent mountain, was seen as a sign that they were constructing a bunker. Also, they should have stopped when ordered to do so. All of this was true, but still they were unarmed. While we were some distance from them when first contact was made, we very well could have run them down. Did they really need to die? I now don't think so. Just another thing that adds to the guilt I sometimes feel about the war.

The following morning (*July 25th*) we air assaulted out of LZ Ollie, landing on a mountain top to our southeast, which was not far from where we had engaged the enemy on June 21st. The mountain was quite high and steep by Vietnam standards, and from its top one could see far into the Bồng Son Plains and out to the South China Sea.

I recall that a Swiss reporter was with us, and therefore believed what was really going on was one fat PR mission, staged to impress him on our efforts in defeating the enemy. The whole Company air assaulted in, but only the 1st and 3rd, were to hump, taking different directions down the mountain and spending the day patrolling. The 2nd Platoon and Mortar Platoon would be staying with the Company CP to provide security. The Swiss reporter stayed with us. Based on our splitting into individual platoons, one could surmise that our mission was, as usual, search and destroy. I don't recall any specific intelligence concerning what was going on in the area other than its proximity to the location of the June 21st battle. If Intelligence suspected it as being a particularly hot area, I would have heard something on the radio.

Our patrol started by descending the mountain, which proved to be particularly difficult. The terrain was quite steep, with elephant grass reaching high over our heads; both of which make it hard to keep our footing. This resulted in numerous papercuts created by the sharp elephant grass. We were eventually forced to work our way into a drainage and continue our downhill descent. To add to our misery, it was also extremely hot. Fortunately for us the drainage was running some water and was quite shaded. At some point, we took advantage of the opportunity this provided by stopping, filling our canteens, and opening C-rations for a lunch break. I do recall one of the guys thought he smelled Mary Jane (*weed, pot*), but I don't recall us taking specific heed. Marijuana was not uncommon. I had previously been told that the North Vietnamese and Viet Cong frequently used it, much in the same manner as out drinking a can of beer. Could be true, don't know. I do not recall why this time we didn't take heed, other than a lot of things in Vietnam smell like pot when burning. Halfway into our lunch break, several heard what sounded like someone chambering a round into a rifle. This did cause the alert to go up, but when nothing happened, we soon resumed half-stepping, BSing and getting some needed rest. Little did we know that we were sitting next to a major encampment of the 17th Battalion 18th Regiment of North Vietnamese Regulars. The signs were all there, running water, overhead canopy and fairly close proximity to the villages below.

We finished our lunch break and worked our way out of the drainage we had been following. At this point, my ability to pinpoint our location would become vitally important. For at the time little did we know that in just a matter of minutes we would be facing a sizable force of North Vietnamese, and the knowledge of our exact location and conveying this to the Company Commander would be essential to our survival.

Our position in relation to the map we were working from was hard to identify. I wouldn't say we were lost; it was just that I could not exactly pinpoint how far down the mountain and drainage we had traveled. This needed to be corrected. The map we were using had us located on its border with an adjacent map, or were we on the adjacent map? I wasn't sure. To add to the difficulty, high tree canopy prevented my observation of adjacent mountain tops from which our location could be fixed. To correct this situation, a soldier was sent up a tree, and an artillery battery was then contacted, requesting that they fire a round of Wiley Peter (*White Phosphorous*). The soldier in the tree was then able to observe the impact of the round and point to its direction, thus giving me a line of reference. Using this and observing an identifiable object in the valley below, two intersecting lines were drawn on our map. The point where these two lines intersected represented our exact location, which was then passed on to the Company Commander. This simple act was repeated numerous times while in Vietnam.

All of this took place following lunch and shortly after we made our way out of the steep-walled drainage. The terrain opened up into a wide channel with shallow sides, and a somewhat gentle downhill slope all of which covered by a brilliant blue sky and a welcomed slight breeze. It looked like we had finally caught a break and the rest of the day would be a cakewalk down to the Bồng Sơn Plains approximately three miles below. The area was blanketed by scattered brush and trees; however, the adjacent ridge did appear to be sufficiently covered with high overhead canopy. Sgt. Edelman's squad resumed the lead, with a soldier by the name of Jones again taking point.

Not long after resuming our decent Edelman worked his way back in the column and informed Lt. Barret that he had just crossed a well-used trail that appeared to parallel the drain and our current route of decent. He was concerned about the columns vulnerability to an ambush posed by this parallel trail and sought permission to halt the Platoon. Edelman, a Texas country boy, was an extremely competent Squad Leader, and his opinions were well respected. If he was concerned, assurance was needed that the column was in no danger. The Lieutenant agreed to the investigation, and Edelman, together with one of his fire teams, pulled out while the rest of us sat in place. He couldn't have been gone more than a few minutes when we heard intense shooting originating four or five hundred yards to our front, left flank, and over the ridge separating us from the next drainage. We knew instantly that it was Edelman and that he was in trouble.

Upon hearing the shooting, Lt. Barret had me contact the Company Commander, who contacted Battalion HQ, informing them of the situation. Most likely, they, in turn, contacted the Air Force; however, I'm not sure who contacted them or where in the sequence of events this contact took place, but the Air Force would soon show up. We didn't immediately receive artillery support for reasons I can now only guess. One can assume that we were too far down into the drainage, thus preventing a good gun angle, or we may have been on gun target line or out of 105 range. But I'm getting ahead of myself.

Led by the remainder of Edelman's squad, together with Lieutenant Barret (*Big Skinny*) and myself, and possibly a few others, we started off in the direction of the shooting. The rest of the Platoon was close behind. We climbed out of the valley and continued to the top of the next ridge, where we met what was left of Edelman's fire team. The majority of the Platoon remained here while the rest of us ran a short distance down the other side. Why the whole Platoon didn't come rushing in, I do not recall. Most likely, the Lieutenant ordered them to take a defensive position on the top of the rise. I do recall that the total number of us descending into harm's way was not very many. Once cresting the ridge and descending the other side we too came under intense rifle fire, which brought us to an immediate halt and scrambling for cover. From here we could observe Edelman lying in the open approximately thirty yards further down the hill and separated from its bottom by another fifteen yards. The shooting came from an area just on the other side of the ravine and about thirty yards from where Edelman was lying. Unfortunately, cover was sparse, while there was an abundance of brush; it afforded nothing that would stop a bullet. There were a few trees of various sizes, but mostly these were small and scattered. They too offered little protection.

The Lieutenant and I dove for the same tree for cover. I won the race, and he pulled up close behind me. We just looked at each other and smiled, each knowing what had just happened. It was one of those "got-ya" humorous moments that can happen even in the direst situation. Yes, there can be humorous moments which will bring a smile even during a firefight. Without saying anything, I slipped off my radio and placed it up close to the tree where it was afforded maximum protection from incoming rifle fire. After which I looked back at him and with no expression what-so-ever on my face and proclaimed that the radio was more important than either of us. He just smiled back, not daring to ask me to trade positions. Yes, while rank does have its privileges, this wasn't one of them. Thinking back on it, I was the one who was snookered—he was now using me like a shield; (*That son-of-a-gun*) with the Lieutenant becoming one of my close friends.

We were without a doubt in a tight spot, pinned down, with nothing but small brush and a few small trees for cover. The exception to this was a couple of larger trees, one being the one which the Lt. and I had jumped behind, and the other a larger tree located 15–20 feet to my right front, behind which Russo, our 79-grenade man, took cover. From this position, he was able to bounce 79 grenade rounds off other trees and bring great harm on the enemy below. Also, at this point we had the Air Force on the horn. Some of the time the Lieutenant was on the radio, most of the time it was me. Immediately upon their arrival, the fighter pilots (*there were two*) were able to identify our position and that of the enemy. Unfortunately, we were too close to one another for the planes to drop their ordinance. Therefore, we had to find a way to get some distance between us and the opposing force. This was not possible, we were tightly pinned down, and a withdrawal was, for the time, out of the question. The shooting from both sides was intense, with green tracers bouncing all around us. Charlie had us wiped, dead to rights. Heavily outnumbered, our only chance being a withdrawal; but how? Then there was the retrieval of Sgt. Edelman. We would not pull back until he was retrieved.

We all realized the predicament we were in tightly pinned down by superior force with no way to get out. While yes, we were in a tight spot, but it wasn't our biggest problem; that being how to recover our comrade, Edelman, be he dead or alive. At this point, we didn't know. Edelman himself provided the answer to this question, with him shouting up to us that we had better hurry and get him out because he was bleeding out. This brought intense pressure on the rest of us to do something. Then out of the blue, Reynard, a member of Edelman's squad, dropped his web gear and started running down to where Edelman was lying. This was done without a spoken word, comment, or order from the Lieutenant. He just started running, which took us all by surprise. There was nothing we could do other than "pop smoke." Which I believed all did followed by opening up with covering fire. The entire area was engulfed in mixed red and green haze that resulted from the exploding smoke canisters. It worked because the next thing we knew, here was Reynard, scrambling up the hill, with Edelman on his back. There wasn't an enemy shot fired as they made their hasty retreat. It was the single most showing of heroism witnessed during my entire tour of duty. I don't think Reynard, who was really a quiet, somewhat unimposing, reserved guy, ever got his just reward or credit for the action he took that day. He was awarded a Bronze Star while the Lieutenant, who was a really good Platoon Leader, but did nothing other than his job got a Silver Star—you see rank really does have its privileges.

As Reynard, packing Edelman, passed our position, we joined in behind him in a hasty retreat to the relative safety offered by the top of the ridge. I joined in as they passed only to become tangled in some low overhanging brush and limbs that brought me to an abrupt stop. A soldier by the name of Greco freed me, and over the rise we went. Once cresting the ridge, actually while on its top, we joined the rest of the platoon and took up defensive positions.

We all safely reached the crest of the hill and the relative safety of the ridge top; however, being severely outnumbered the outcome of this day was still very much in doubt. Except for now being on the high ground offered by the ridge, the situation had little changed; we were still pinned in place by enemy fire. We were 20+ against what seemed to be the world. However, on the positive side, enough separation between us had now been established for us to receive some degree of air support. Unfortunately, this was limited to strafing the area to our immediate front. The pilots desperately wanted to provide more help but couldn't. They would have us pop smoke to mark our line and again bemoan their heartfelt regret for not being able to provide greater assistance due to the tightness of the opposing forces. While they were unable to drop their ordinance (booms) on the enemy; they were able to strafe their position which would momentarily bring the shooting to a stop, with both sides deciding that keeping one's head down was the prudent thing to do.

At some point Lt. Barret in concert with the pilots decided to have napalm dropped on our lower right flank (southern flank) and on the adjacent hill to our left rear (south by southeast), thus stopping any attempt on the enemy's part from attacking our flank. We were now somewhat ringed on two sides by a wall of fire, scorching the jungle no more than approximately 150 to 200 yards from our location. The heat originating from this together with the smell of burning gas engulfed our little ridge top. Shrapnel created by the exploding napalm canisters bounced all around us, and for a short while this posed a bigger threat than incoming rifle fire. Only one G.I. was hit by fragments from a napalm canister; fortunately, he wasn't badly hurt, just a piece of hot metal between his pack and back. While I was amazed at how fast he could shed his pack, I was more amazed that he hardly had a scratch on him.

By using my helmet to cover the radio and my body to cover Edelman, each were afforded some protection from incoming shrapnel. Edelman was in quite a bit of pain and also had lost a large amount of blood. Because of the blood loss, Docimo, our platoon medic, was reluctant to administer morphine. But he soon decided it was better to take a chance on sticking him with a tube of morphine than to have him go into a shock-induced coma. Docimo had previously administered a tourniquet to his wounded leg which controlled the bleeding. This too resulted in concern, should it be loosened, or left alone? I believe it was kept in place.

At about this same time, the First Platoon was able to contact us. They took up a position on the adjoining mountainside located to the west by southwest, and when facing uphill, they were to our left, approximately 400 to 500 yards away. Unfortunately, the Company Commander and the Mortar Platoon also tried to link up, but to no avail. All they accomplished was getting people hurt.

Finally, the pilots informed us that they had done all they could and would be returning to their base to refuel. However, they would stick around long enough to provide us some support during our breakout from the ridge top.

It was decided that if we were to survive, we had to disengage, link up with the First Platoon and make our way back up the mountain from which we came. The order finally came from the Company Commander, after considerable consultation with Big Skinny for us to break out. However, this would not be a simple task. Our path for making such a retreat was now blocked by the enemy. After a bunch of Bang, Bang, and shoot-em-up, a small opening in the enemy line was achieved.

Sgt. Allen, our Platoon Sgt., was positioned behind a Puerto Rican kid, named Rivera, who was to be actual point on our attempting to break contact and get the hell out of there. Unfortunately, Rivera was wounded when Sgt. Allen threw a grenade up the hill at the enemy position, preventing our departure. The grenade sadly rolled back, and upon exploding, fragments hit Rivera. Things like that all too often happen. Sgt. Allen had a hard time shaking the thought that he had been so foolish as to throw a grenade uphill. Rivera, being badly hurt, along with Edelman, would now have to be carried all the way up the mountain. Rivera was a tough little guy; I liked and respected him a lot. Our boys were soon able to eliminate the enemy blocking our route of escape thus allowing for us to link up with the First Platoon; whereupon they took point. This was good, thus allowing the employment of Third Platoon boys in the carrying out of their own wounded and leaving the responsibility of the point to the First Platoon. If memory serves me right, we had in all three, maybe four wounded, with two having to be carried while the third and possibly the fourth were walking. Time has taken its toll on my memory, and I just can't recall the exact numbers. I do know we remarkably had no fatalities.

Greco, the kid who had previously untangled me while making our escape over the ridge, was slightly grazed on the cheek or chin during the first stage of the firefight. He was just slightly touched. A matter of a fraction of an inch separated him from receiving a scratch and that of having his jaw blown off, just a matter of a fraction of an inch. Life in Vietnam was funny that way. He was ok and walked out. He was another good kid. The soldier (*I do not recall who it was*) that had the hot shrapnel from the exploding napalm canisters lodge between his pack and back suffered only minor burns.

At this point, we were successful in our attempt to link up with the First Platoon. As for the 2nd, I don't know where they were. The Captain in company with the Mortar Platoon tried unsuccessfully to link up. Bad idea! It is doubtful that they could have offered much in the line of help. This was the second time the Mortar Platoon was wasted on a fool's journey by the same Company Commander in little more than a month. Unfortunately, they were hit, being unaware that they were walking straight into the mess. A couple of the boys were wounded, including the guy that had been given my rifle, following my getting wounded back on June 21st. The Mortar Platoon dropped and destroy their mortar tubes as they beat a hasty retreat back up the mountain. The guy with my old rifle, upon getting wounded dropped it and it was undoubtedly picked up by the enemy. In later discussion, we found this quite amusing. Both the mortarman and I got wounded while carrying this same rifle. The rifle was definitely bad luck, a taboo, a jinx. Anyone carrying it was going to get shot. Oh, that poor, unsuspecting North Vietnamese soldier was in for a rude awaking. Yes, this became part of our nightly discussion while drinking C-ration coffee. It always brought on a chuckle.

Counting Greco, I believe there were three for sure and possibly four wounded in our platoon and a couple more in the Mortar Platoon. I recall for sure that Rivera and Edelman, being the more seriously wounded, were carried out, the others had to walk. Having two on improvised stretchers meant that eight riflemen had to be assigned to the task of carrying them. The platoon normally had about 24 to 28 in all, (*I don't recall the exact number that day*) which begs the question, who was available for stretcher bearer duty. The Platoon Leader and Platoon Sgt., two M-60 machine guns, two ammo bearers, 2 RTOs, and of course a point man would be unavailable for this task. Add to this two wounded and possibly two walking wounded, that's approximately 13 unable to be utilized as stretcher-bearers. This duty would then fall on the thirteen remaining. Eight of these were immediately assigned as bearers; thus, leaving only about five who would be available as relief bearers as well as being available for carrying all the extra gear. No wonder the Platoon needed help to carry out wounded. This is the only time I had hard feelings for the Company, especially members of the 1st Platoon who were reluctant to help us carry our wounded.

The Second Platoon met us as we moved to about three-quarters of the way up the mountain and helped with the wounded and packing gear. At one point their Platoon Sgt. put Edelman on his back to scale some rocks and ascend a particularly steep section of our ascent. For his effort he severely hurt his back and never returned to the field. As for us, we eventually made it to the top at about 4 a.m., whereupon we dropped our gear in exhaustion and fell asleep upon the ground.

I mentioned that during the first part of the firefight we didn't have artillery cover. This all changed once the Air Force pulled out and we made our initial extraction, pulling ourselves out of the lower drainage area and climbing up onto a higher ridge. The departure of the Air Force and the introduction of artillery support were almost simultaneous. We maintained our position on an ascending ridge-line, following it all the way back to the top of the hill. It was a journey that took many hours and lasted well into the early hours of the next day. Once the artillery support kicked in, it was with us all night, not stopping until we reached the relative safety of the mountain top. This blows my earlier assumption that we may have been out of 105 range. But, as I think back on it, it was those big track guns, 175s that fired support all night, not 105s. It had to be our location and gun target line that prevented their early support, that together with the arrival of the Air Force. This reinforces the importance of knowing one's exact location in relation to a Papa Oscar. If I had misrepresented our location and artillery did kick in, and if we were on gun target line, they could have been shooting directly into our position. As stated, I did earlier talk to an artillery group, and they were able to fire a round some distance off to our flank. And, from this, I was able to affirm our exact location.

During the actual break out, neither Lieutenant Barret nor I were involved in directing artillery support. It must have been coming from the Lieutenant of the 1st Platoon or the Company Commander who was located on the mountain top. I don't believe I've ever given this any thought until just now. *Who was calling in the artillery? I don't know.* I now doubt it was the 1st Platoon, if it was, I would have heard it on the radio. Well maybe not, they could have been using the artillery push. Anyway, we did receive artillery support the remainder of the night. A whole lot of BOOM! BOOM! Directed not only to cover our retreat but to annihilate the enemy position.

The next morning, we were extracted back to Uplift, where we stayed and rested the remaining day. A couple of us did take the opportunity to walk over to the artillery platoon that provided us covering support all night and thanked them for their effort. Eventually, they were given some of the NVA weaponry policed up by another company that was assigned cleanup duty following our extraction. Normally a company that was in the shit isn't asked to clean it up.

As for the unlucky reporter who had been assigned to tag along with us. He was a Swiss fellow who had just left Israel, covering the Six-Day War. His assignment at the time was with an Egyptian unit that was forced to run in retreat the whole time he was with them. Fortunately, for us, his English was quite good. I guess you would have to say, "he was just bad luck, a jinx." For a time while we were pinned down on the ridge, we really didn't know how it was going to turn out. Charlie had us wiped. He just didn't know it. At this point, the Swiss reporter took Edelman's M16 and joined the fray. We couldn't resist kidding and laughed with him about being a part of a forever-neutral Swiss Army, and this being the first time a Swiss military officer was shooting at someone in over a hundred years. And again, he was on the run. Humor can take place even in the direst situations. We found the situation the Swiss man had got himself into quite amusing. We never let up on the poor guy while the shooting was going on. He too chuckled with us over this. I've often wondered what happened to him. I later learned that he did write an account of what took place that day, but I've never seen or read it. I doubt that he gave us a glowing review.

An interesting side note concerns one of the pilots flying support for us that day. As luck would have it, my parents were in Thailand at the time, with my Dad working for Utah Construction, who was contracted to build Air Force runways in Northern Thailand. Mom, as usual, tagged along, and to pass the time took a job in a PX at one of these airbases. It just so happened that the airplanes flying support for us that day were from this same base. Within hours of returning to their base, one of the pilots was at the PX and of all things, talking to my mom. While he had no idea that the soldier, he was just talking to over in Vietnam was, in fact, the son of the lady at the PX; all he knew was that she had a son who was with the 1ˢᵗ of the 5ᵗʰ, 1ˢᵗ Cav. He relayed to her the problems he had just encountered while flying this mission for this unit. Mom later informed me of this conversation, confirming that in fact, it was I, her son, to whom he was talking with not more than a couple of hours earlier.

DRANK TOO MUCH

Jul 31ˢᵗ Surrounded a village— killed 1 VC. Walked late into night.
Set up in an area we were in before.
Aug 1ˢᵗ Left for Uplift.
Aug 2ⁿᵈ 1 KIA Made an air assault into burned out village—killed 1
VC & captured 2 more. Evacuated refugees.
Aug 3ʳᵈ Nothing. Laid around Uplift.

Following the firefight of July 25ᵗʰ, we were extracted to Uplift for a couple of days of rest and recuperation. Thinking they were giving us a couple days off, Lt. Barret and I decided to tie one on. He, being an officer, was entitled to a bottle of whiskey from his ration card. Enlisted men and NCOs had no such privileges. After he got hold of a bottle of Kentucky's best, we settled down to watch a movie, which I believe was *The Ten Commandments* and downed that bottle. My last recollection is falling between the logs that formed the movie viewers seats, lying there, not wanting to move. Somehow my buddies managed to carry me back to the hole we were sleeping in, and there I spent the night, oblivious to the world. Still don't know how *The Ten Commandments* ends.

The Army always seems to know how to ruin a good thing. I was awoken early the next morning with the worst hangover I had while in Vietnam. Thinking back on it, I believe it was the only time I got really that drunk while in Vietnam. Shaking, my head pounding, I got ready to move out on a patrol through an area that was the site of a major firefight some months before. I sure didn't want to go, but if the Lieutenant could muster the energy to get us moving, then I could muster the energy to make the patrol. This sort of outing usually amounts to nothing more than a walk through the woods, but of course this time it had to be different. Shortly after the choppers had set us on the ground, we made contact with a lone gunman. This guy must have been having a rougher day than I. As we approached what was thought to be an abandoned hooch, he comes running out with a U.S. Colt 1911, 45 blazing. Docimo, our medic was his primary target. Docimo pulls out his 45 and pulls the trigger. Nothing happens, the 45 froze up, leaving the medic in a very untenable position. He took refuge behind a palm tree as our point man, Boharkas, seeing the plight of the medic, raised his M16, pulls the trigger, again nothing happens, except having all the cartridges falling out the bottom of its magazine onto the ground. I was some distance *(maybe 30 to 40 feet)* off to the side, watching this comedy of errors play out. Boharkas's actions sidetracked the determined Viet Cong giving the medic time to get his 45 back into working order. Now, still hiding behind the tree, he was able to shoot and take down the aggressor. All this shooting resulted in my head exploding, pounding me into submission. I just sat down on a log and waited for this mess to be cleared up. The Lieutenant came over, face in hands, and sat next to me. The only words spoken: "Can you believe this shit?"

It wasn't long before we were up and walking, working our way closer to the coast. I was dragging along, not wanting to speak to anyone, just trying to get through the day. Sure enough, Bang, Bang, some son-of-a-bitch was again shooting at us. I wasn't far from Parks and watched as he jumped behind this little tiny twig of a bush that provided him absolutely no cover what-so-ever. Here's this big 200 pounder trying to hide behind this little twig. He really looked so silly. I just looked down and kept on walking. Parks emphatically yelling at me, "Mac, get down! We are taking incoming fire!"

Still, I kept walking, responding as I continued on my way, "Let the little bastard put me out of my misery." Getting down would have proven to be just too painful, my head wouldn't take the jerking reaction. I feared that once I got down, I wouldn't ever be able to get back up. They would just have had to bury me in place. Fortunately, our boys were quick to return fire, which brought about an end to Charlie's shooting. Within a few minutes we worked our way into the nearby village which sat not more than fifty yards from the South China Sea and rounding up two of the bad guys. It was the worst day spent in Oz.

Two things happened that day that I hesitate to put to paper: The first involves the shooting of the VC by Docimo that I mentioned earlier. As this young VC was lying on the ground, probably dying from his wound (*but maybe not*), one of our boys walked over to him and proceeded to put three or four more rounds into the poor fellow. With every burst, the gook twitched and turned in a death spasm. With each subsequent burst from his M16, this fellow shouts at the dying man, "Die you son-of-a-bitch, die." I remember thinking at the time that this tragic picture was in some way humorous. I had regressed that far. The thought of my finding humor in the events unfolding before me, the tragic death of another human, continues to trouble me.

The second incident that troubles me is, after finally making our way to the coast and rounding up the two or three suspected VCs we called in the South Vietnamese police (*a semi-military unit of the South Vietnamese government*). They, in turn, took charge of the VC suspects and walked some fifty yards further down the beach and began interrogating them. The process of interrogation involved having one of the suspects squatting before the interrogator, who then began beating the poor fellow with a bamboo stick across his shins. These weren't love taps but full force whacks across the shins.

I, along with the rest of those that had gathered, could not help but witness the beating. We began talking among ourselves, expressing our beliefs that this was just wrong. We didn't capture these guys just to hand them over to the South Vietnamese and then witness their torture. Walking over to Lt. Barret, I informed him that the boys were getting worked up and if the beating didn't stop, things were going to rapidly get out of hand. Knowing that I had the backing of the rest of the platoon, I turned from Lt. Barret and started walking to where the beating was taking place with the full intent of putting a stop to it. After only a couple of steps, I felt Lt. Barret's hand on my shoulder. "Hold up Mac, I'll take care of it," which he did. Soon after that choppers were there, and we were lifted back to Uplift

I now find it very strange that in a relatively short period I could digress to the point where I found humor in death, while a short time later, I was so full of compassion. Very strange, I can't explain it. The best I can do is acknowledge that the beast resides within us all and it can get out of control. When placed in a situation that is contrary to all one has been taught, one must recognize this, and find what remnant of humanity still resides within, call upon it to keep that beast bottled up. Again, James Fennimore Cooper's, explanation of humanity in a wilderness setting as stated in *The Leather Stocking Tales* was oh so right. My life while serving in Vietnam was full of contradictions. Good/evil, what's first thought to be black can often be white, and what one is raised to believe as abysmal, an unforgiven sin is okay, acceptable. Go figure? Was Vietnam truly my Cumberland Gap?

What makes this even more troubling is that by this time in my tour, I was becoming both figuratively and in actuality the "Old Man" of the Platoon. Being twenty-six at the time put me in a position of being the oldest enlisted man of the unit. Many of the younger, as well as newly arrived G.I.s often looked to me to give some assurance of their survival, comfort during troubled times, on occasion spiritual guidance in their private lives and to provide assurance that they would make it home. I was at times amazed at what they would, in the strictest of confidence, convey. I never betrayed their trust. The officers and senior non-commissioned officers (sergeants), as well as I, recognized this strange position I held in the Platoon. One in which I had to be careful of what I did and said. For example, I didn't whore around. The younger guys were watching to see if I would fail in taking the higher moral ground. If asked, I would represent them and their grievances to the ranking authority of the platoon. As the old man of the platoon, my opinion was respected, and on occasion sought out by the company leadership. This influence over some of the other men almost got me into trouble midway through my tour while in a gunfight in what is referenced the "Rock Pile" and my yelling, without thinking to my good friend Irving to shoot a wounded NVA soldier. Fortunately for me he didn't. I guess the beast within got a little out of control. It could happen.

COMPANY COMES DOWN WITH CHOLERA

Aug 4th Made 2 air assaults and secured for the landing of an APC
& air assaulted to the top of a Mnt. and walked down. VERY HOT.
Aug 5th Did Nothing. Laid around Uplift.
Aug 6th Leave Uplift for Hawaneye (LZ Bird).
Aug. 7th Sick–lay around. Leave tomorrow for Pony then a 2-day
trek through woods.
Aug 8th The whole Co sick. Left for Pony about 4pm. 6pm started
humping—men fell out with cramps. Plt. down to 13 men. Turn
back.
Aug 9th Stayed at Pony the night. Mission abandoned. Will leave
for Uplift to secure 13 men left in Plt.
Aug 10th At Uplift this morning. The Plt. took showers and washed
their clothes.
Aug 11th Took over perimeter guard at Uplift bunkers 31-34.

Disease and illness can take its toll. On August 6th, we air assaulted into an abandoned firebase called LZ Bird located in the Kim Son Valley, a notoriously hostile area. The former firebase had been overrun by North Vietnamese regulars six to eight months earlier. I recall the weather being unsettled, raining, while at the same time being hot and humid. A rain squall would roll in, giving us a drenching, leaving us wet and cold only to be followed by a clear hot sky. You could feel the humidity rising from the jungle floor. Being wet and cold, followed by then basking in the hot sun always made me sleepy, but then, we were almost always tired from lack of sleep.

Upon arrival at the abandoned base, we set up our defenses utilizing what was left of its fortification. Our air mattresses were laid out, and mosquito nets hung in the somewhat destroyed perimeter bunkers. Patrols were then run out of here for a couple of days. Upon returning early one afternoon from one of these outings, I proceeded to crawl onto my air mattress with the intent of catching a couple of Zs as part of well-deserved afternoon nap. A mosquito net was stretched across a ring of sandbags affording some protection from all manner of flying pests. The sun had come out drying us off from the soaking received from the morning squall, and I was quite comfortable in my slumber. The sound of laughter soon woke me from my all too short nap. Looking up, the bright sun was shining directly down upon me, warming my wet body while at the same time blinding my sight.

The laughter continued, but I couldn't determine what the hell was so damn funny. My eyes slowly began to focus on a bunch of my close friends, just standing there, staring down, waiting for me to react. I soon came to understand the reason for the commotion. A three-foot snake had trapped itself on top of my mosquito net. It would wiggle and twist, coil and stretch out, attempting to escape, only to roll back down into the sagging net. The net with the snake on top was now no more than a foot from my nose. Evidently, my friends thought this to be quite funny. I did not. I was out of there in a flash. Once I gathered my wits, I laid into all of them that were within reach. That only intensified the laughter. "OK you bastards, I will extract revenge." Then we all had a good laugh on me. As for the snake, some of the boys were able to get it off the net and dispose of it. Almost all snakes in Vietnam are extremely venomous.

The next day I came down with a high fever. It generally took a 102 temperature to get you sent back to a MASH unit for treatment. I guess my fever hadn't reached that point for I wasn't sent back, but stayed there in the abandoned firebase, while some of the Platoon went out on patrol. It only lasted a day and night, followed by full recovery. Shortly after that we were picked up and flown to LZ Pony where that evening, we were going to mount a Company sized patrol up into the adjacent mountains, leaving the LZ as the sun faded. It was estimated that we would be walking a couple of nights and a couple of days, before reaching our destination, which was suspected to be a heavily entrenched NVA base area.

We began our march on schedule, leaving Pony under the cover of darkness and crossing a fairly deep river, and then gradually ascending the adjacent mountain. Around eight p.m., our guys started falling out, sick with stomach cramps and violent vomiting. This happened over and over forcing our assault onto the mountain to grind to a halt. The medics were trying to treat twenty, thirty, and then forty men all on the ground. Our line was strung out for what seemed to be a half mile. The Company Commander was beside himself, not wanting to abandon the mission, but the medics were insisting on sending back the sick, which had in less than a one-hour period, seriously reduced the number of his command. Obviously, the mission had to be scrubbed. Now how to get everyone back to LZ Pony and try to figure out what had happened. Eventually, this was achieved by deploying a convoy of trucks, which connected with us along a stretch of a dirt road that paralleled the river we had previously crossed. This in itself was quite dangerous, trucks on the road in a very hostile area at night. We carried the sick down off the mountain and onto the waiting convoy, then rode back to LZ Pony where the battalion surgeon was waiting.

The following day a medical unit examined those that hadn't been hospitalized the night before. After some time, a determination was made that we had encountered some form of Cholera, which literally and physically scared the shit out of us all. Four of the company were so seriously sick; they had to be flown to Japan for treatment. Interestingly, the Philippines refused to allow the flight carrying these boys permission to land. They eventually reconsidered and allowed the refueling. As for the abandoned mission up into the mountains, another sister company took our place. They eventually did run into the enemy, resulting in a major firefight that took the lives of several of their guys. The Cholera was bad enough, but the guilt of having another company take our place and them getting seriously hurt made it doubly hard to take.

A couple of weeks later we were again out in the boonies patrolling. As the company was setting up for the night, hot chow was flown in. Shortly following the landing of our evening meal, small groups were directed to the area where the meal was to be served and once there form a chow line. It was finally my turn to leave my fox hole and join the line and get some hot food. Upon approaching the area, I noticed that the new arrivals were being lined up by platoon and those arriving ahead of me were standing in line with their pants down, bare bottoms shining in the evening sunlight while the platoon medics administered shots. There, out in the middle of the jungle, miles from any form of civilization, stood a bunch of men bare-assed. What a scene it was. One had to see it to grasp the absurdity and humor of the moment. It just wasn't something you see every day. I watched as the medics performed their respective duty. A G.I. would walk up, bend over and the medic would insert the needle. For the shot to work it had to be administered into a bloodstream. The medic would insert the needle then pull back the plunger. If pink, he would then inject the serum. They didn't always pull back pink, in which case he would reinsert the needle and repeat the process. For some unknown reason my medic, Docimo, was having a hard time pulling back pink. Some of my poor comrades were repeatably injected time and time again. Observing this, I decided maybe it was best if I joined in the line of one of the other platoons. Never did mention this to Docimo, didn't want to hurt his feelings.

WOUNDED BY FRIENDLY FIRE

*Aug 12th Went out with tanks to 506 Valley. Got hit by shrapnel.
Aug 13th Moved out into the field. Night ambush. Same area as in
March.*

You'd be surprised, or perhaps you wouldn't, at how many of our troops were hurt by friendly fire. It's not hard to understand when considering how many boys are out there armed to the hilt, and how easy it is to accidentally walk into one another. A short-lived firefight would ensue, and in short order, it would be realized what had just happened, and order would be restored. Unfortunately, men got hurt; some died. In the heat of a close-up firefight, air support has a hard time identifying the good guys from the enemy; in such cases bad things can happen. A guy that was assigned to the Mongoose at the same time as Parks and me, by the name of Temple shot and killed himself while riding in a jeep. The jeep hit a rough spot and Temple's rifle went off, killing him. Another low quarter (*a guy not in the infantry*) was fascinated with one of our guy's Colt 1911, 45. As he was playing around with it, not knowing it was cocked and loaded, he accidentally shot another guy right in the chest, killing him instantly. As indicated during the firefight in August, when Sgt. Edelman got hit, we had the Air Force dropping napalm canisters into our position, and a piece of shrapnel hit one of our guys. Back in March, the same day I was almost hit by a booby-trapped 105 round, another company of U.S. troops was entrenched a short distance from us. Neither Company had any knowledge of the others close proximity, and they unknowingly launched a couple of mortar rounds into our position. It wasn't until the next morning that this mess was straightened out. While in this same area we were set up for the night. Along about dark thirty a trooper decided he had to relieve himself and walked out in front of the perimeter to take care of his business. He failed to tell the person on guard in the adjacent hole that he was going out front. Upon his return to his fox hole he was shot and killed, believing he was an enemy soldier trying to infiltrate our line. I guess the only way I can explain this is to acknowledge that shit does happen. One platoon can be patrolling in an area unaware that another group of G.I.s are also in the same area. When they accidentally meet, all hell can break out. Case in point, my good friend Curtis was wounded when a platoon from our own Company walked into my platoon while patrolling in thick jungle, A short firefight broke out between us before anyone realized what was happening. As a result, Curtis was hit. In another close call we heard voices off in the distance and immediately set up an ambush. As it turned out a small LRRP patrol was headed straight into the ambush. Fortunately, we were able to recognize them and make contact before bad things had a chance to happen.

On August 12th we were accompanying a couple of tanks (*maybe it was just one*) while patrolling up the 506 Valley. Not much was happening, and we were kicked back enjoying the ride. Someone spotted what appeared to be a fortified position, and it was decided to shoot a couple of M79 rounds into it before we climbed in and checked it out. Just as one of the M79 grenades went off, I felt a painful burning in my right shoulder. I'd been hit by a piece of shrapnel, suffering my second wound. (*No Purple Heart for this one*) Fortunately, I wasn't badly hurt, and I still carry this small piece of shrapnel in my shoulder to this day. Strangely, I was in the process of taking a picture of the guy as he shot his M79 Grenade Launcher. I, therefore, possess a picture of a guy shooting me.

I have no idea how many men were killed in Vietnam from friendly fire, but I imagine it is a sobering number.

BATTLE OF THE ROCK PILE

Aug 14th Looking for a battalion—false report. Walked hard. Didn't find a thing. Climbed to the top of a hill and set up for the night.
Aug 15th Dropped our packs with mortars and humped to a ridge-line where we could see 1.6 & 2.6. Moved back. That night hard hump. Set up alone.
Aug 17th 6 months in Vietnam (half over.) Searched our way back up—linked up with CP Lose 1 WIA & 2 KIA. Pulled back & called in airstrike. Pulled blocking force that night.
Aug 18th Called in more airstrikes & 8-inch guns. Dropped gas, moved back up into the rocks & searched them out—got 4 gooks, 1 wounded. Spent night in the lower ground.
Aug 19th Air assaulted—suspected Co in area. Same area we have been working in. Walked downhill and set up.
Aug 20th Extracted to LZ Pony—fed breakfast. Drank beer with ARVNS.

Some people won't walk under a ladder, others will walk around a block to avoid crossing a black cat. Taboos just have a way of working themselves into our psyche. This is especially true of men in combat. To me, it always appeared things went bad during the bottom half of a month. This was especially true if by chance Parks was able, for some bullshit reason, to worm his way out of the field, leaving me alone to save the world. If by chance these were happening in conjunction, shit was going to hit the fan.

This time it started with us being told that we were being committed into an area where a suspected sizable North Vietnamese force was located. A captured NVA soldier told of a company size group of North Vietnamese regulars holding up in a bunch of natural caves formed by car-sized boulders piled one atop another. This soldier would accompany us into the suspected area. Oh yes, this was the latter part of the month, and Parks would shortly leave the field. The stars were aligning, Bad things were about to happen—no doubt, and we all knew it.

It all started innocent enough; however, our flight and landing were in itself, something unusual. An attempt to fool the enemy would be undertaken which involved our touching down or making false landings on several sites. Eventually, the landing zone was reached, at which point the choppers hovered a few feet from the ground, forcing us to jump almost on the fly. In this manner the whole company reached and secured the chosen hilltop. Although it was now approaching dusk, the Company moved off the LZ, following a ridgeline some 3 to 4 thousand meters to where we eventually dug in for the night. I remember that the mosquitoes were particularly bad.

Early the next morning, accompanied by the CP (*Company Commander and his surrounding support group*) and with the NVA Soldier in tow, the 3rd Platoon proceeded in its search for the reported NVA Company. At this point, Parks was still with us. The captured soldier was to lead the platoon to where his not so long-ago comrades were holed up. A considerable distance was walked before it was determined our guide had no idea as to the location of his former comrades. After much discussion, the Company Commander decided it was a waste of time for us to continue, and that we should return to where we had spent the previous night. While we were stopped, awaiting this decision, I had a chance to strike up a conversation with the prisoner. It was surprising how well soldiers from different armies and different languages could communicate. Over a couple of smokes, it was learned that this guy was married and from a small village in North Vietnam, north of Hanoi.

One of the many contradictions experienced while in Vietnam, was my feeling of sympathy and a certain comradeship with a North Vietnamese soldier once he was captured. He was no longer the enemy, but just as another soldier that likely would rather have been back home enjoying his family. He was just another poor slob, who like me, was drafted into his Army and truly wished that he hadn't been. Equally strange, I didn't have this same feeling for a captured Viet Cong Soldier. I thought of him as a sneaky little son-of-a-bitch who enjoyed the misery he was inflicting on others; thus, there was no problem in helping him meet his maker.

The march back was punctuated by it being extremely hot, which resulted in one of our boys, a real friendly small black guy, falling out with heatstroke. Now the jig was up, for there was no alternative but to call in a medevac for his extraction. This would surely result in alerting every enemy soldier as to our location. Now, if we were ever to accidentally stumble into the suspected encampment of NVA soldiers, they would be expecting us, and they would have the upper hand.

Once back to our previous night's bivouac area and since our location was well known, it was determined that having DDT flown over us to reduce the number of mosquitoes would do no harm. This was the only time that DDT was ever flown directly over us while I was in Vietnam. So much for Rachel Carson (*Look it up*). Another day in paradise had come to an end with our having humped the boonies, finding nothing, and a fellow soldier falling out and probably never returning to the unit. (*Once one suffers heatstroke, he will in all likelihood succumb to it the next time exposed to extreme heat and extreme fatigue; In which case he would become a liability to the rest of the unit—thus no return*). Later that evening the much-appreciated hot chow was flown in.

Now for the taboo, my buddy Parks, under some pretext, talked the powers to be into letting him return to Base Camp. Parks and another fellow by the name of Temple, caught the same chopper that brought in our evening meal back to An Khê. As for Temple, he was accidentally killed a couple of days later while riding in a jeep and having his rifle discharge when the jeep hit a bump and the bullet striking and killing him.

It was the last quarter of the month, and Parks was not with the rest of us. Things were now ripe for us to be involved in our next big firefight! "The Battle of the Rock Pile."

The next day we retraced our footsteps of the previous day. Now separated from the rest of the Company, including the Company Commander, the Platoon moved along a broken ridgeline until we were able to observe the 1st and 2nd Platoons some distance below moving up on an adjacent ridgeline. Here we set up alone for the night, separated from the rest of the company. Our cuisine for our evening meal: C-rations heated over our makeshift tin can stoves of course. Sitting here as I write this and thinking back on it—I actually liked C-rations.

Early the next morning we found ourselves descending into the coastal lowlands from where we could observe the remainder of the Company working its way down towards our location. With them no more than a quarter of a mile between us, they came into contact originating from a large area of scattered boulders. Three soldiers were down, 2 killed and one wounded. We immediately started moving up the mountain in an attempt to link up. The rock pile was a natural fortification with numerous caves, cracks, and crannies. For reasons I do not recall, my platoon, the 3rd, was way down in strength. We lacked an officer and a Platoon Sergeant, and our total count was no more than 14 or 15. This resulted in my taking on the added responsibility of an acting Squad Leader as well as RTO. Observation choppers were soon in the air, giving them close air observation of the battle area. Our orders were now not to link up but to sweep up into the rock pile and engage the enemy in close combat. *(Just thought of this, we were down to, at the most 16 people, and were to attack a forti-fied enemy position of anticipated company size. What the hell were they thinking? All that saved us was the enemy had no idea as to how many of us made up the attacking force, in addition they were scattered throughout the rock pile area, had limited communication capability, and we were hitting separated, isolated areas. I've never given this any thought until now.)* Either the 1st or 2nd Plt. provided protection for the CP and the other formed a blocking force, closing off any possibility of Charlie escaping up the hill. That left only one platoon, to attack the entrenched enemy, us the 3rd Platoon; all 14 to 16 of us.

We moved up, rock by rock. The firing was intense. At one point a small bubble chopper was flying just a few feet over my right shoulder, directing me to where its pilot observed an NVA soldier squatting behind a large boulder. The pilot of the chopper was directing me to where the NVA was hiding. Finally, I reached the large rock, VC on one side, me on the other, with the pilot directing me to go around the rock and confront and hopefully eliminate the enemy. Lots of luck. I was thinking, *you get out of the chopper and walk around this rock and shoot him!* I decided my best alternative was to get down on my belly and look under the curvature of the rock where it did provide some view of the footing on the other side. My plan was if I did encounter a pair of sandaled feet on the other side, I'd shoot the poor fellow in the foot or leg and then jump around to put on the *coup de grâce*, fortunately, no feet. So, I decided the only thing I could do was just jump around the rock with my M16 blazing. Which I did, but no NVA (*Good!*). It soon became evident that we were not going to be able to dislodge the enemy, who was now pretty well bottled up with little opportunity to escape. (They really had little opportunity to do other than hold their position. They couldn't attack us, even though they outnumbered us by a fairly large number. To do so would require them to expose themselves and thus be subject to being annihilated by air and artillery support.) Their only hope was to try to escape under the cover of darkness—which a number of them eventually did, (leaving their dead and wounded behind.)

Now came time for us to do what we always did best. Drop back and call in the big guns. We moved back to level ground, separating us from the rock pile by some 300 to 400 yards. Now artillery came into play. BOOM, BOOM, with no let up throughout the remainder of the day which was now approaching evening. The artillery continued their barrage all night, stopping only when we made our advance the next morning. The second day was a repeat of the first, with us trying to dislodge the NVA and them holding tight. A lot of shooting with little results. I believe we lost one from the Third Platoon and one wounded, but I'm not sure. We set up again on the lower ground for the night, preventing a downhill escape while the CP, 1st and 2nd remained on the mountainside above the rock pile, maintaining a blocking force further up the mountain. All night long, BOOM, BOOM!

Early next morning, we found ourselves again pushing up the mountain, moving from boulder to boulder. Same as the previous day with the same anticipated results. We could advance so far, but no further. By now, Lt. Barret had rejoined the Platoon; however, our numbers were still quite low. At one point I joined up with a couple other members of the platoon, one by the name of Curtis. He was new, joining the company just in time to take part in the battle of June 21st. He had a Mohawk haircut that made him look like a real badass, which he wasn't. He was a young guy from I believe an area near Pendleton, Oregon. I liked him from the start and have kept in contact with him to this day. Well here was Curtis, dropping down into this large separation of two immense boulders, forming a natural cave at their base. So, down drops Curtis, reaching solid footing eight to ten feet down into the cave. Just as he starts to go around one of the boulders, he is met, face to face with an NVA soldier, no more than a couple of feet away. Curtis is armed with an M79 Grenade Launcher which is loaded with a single shotgun round. He has only this one shot, and then he is out of business except for the Colt 1911—45 on his hip. He stepped back just as the NVA did the same. Curtis extended his arms and directed his M79 around the corner to where the NVA was assumed to be waiting. BOOM. Unfortunately for Curtis, he missed. The NVA soldier extended his arms and unloaded the ten to fifteen rounds from his SKS. I was standing above the hole into which Curtis had just descended.

All I could see was a cloud of dust and the brass shavings emitting from the cavern. Then, up popped Curtis, unwounded, but covered with small scratches created by the brass shavings bouncing off the surrounding rocks. The most damage done resulted from his climbing out of the hole. He wore his fingertips raw attempting to scratch his way up and out. Curtis was visibly shaken. "Shit Mac, he was just standing there, face to face with me. He was as surprised as me." Curtis jumped out of that hole so fast he left behind his empty M79, which was later to cause him some heartburn.

Somewhere around this time, we were again ordered to move back down the mountain to retake the positions we occupied the previous night. But, before we began to move out word came down from the Old Man, who had joined up with the Third Platoon, that he wanted someone (meaning Curtis) to go back down into the hole and retrieve the M79. "Bullshit," was Curtis's response. "I'm not going back down there." And, he didn't. Not until the next day.

While descending the trail leading down the mountain, our point man, a good friend by the name of Irving, a West Virginia boy, yelled back up the line that he had a wounded gook laying in the trail. Without thinking, I yelled back, "Shoot the son-of-a-bitch." Thankfully, Irving had a bigger heart than I. Our descent was now interrupted by the discovery of this wounded North Vietnamese soldier and the question of what to do with him. The word came down from the Old Man to carry the wounded soldier down to where he could be airlifted out. "Irving, you found him, you carry him." Up on Irving's back goes the wounded soldier. The poor fellow died after Irving took only a couple of steps and was left on the trail. By this time the Old Man had moved down to where I was standing. He looked me in the eye and proceeded to let me have it. "Mac, you know you have some influence (actually very limited) on the guys in this platoon. If Irving would have shot that fellow, I would have brought you up on charges." To this day, I don't know if I really meant for Irving to shoot the guy or if I was just blowing off steam. Thank God Irving didn't listen to me.

That evening Parks rejoined the Platoon. I was really glad to see him, but that didn't stop me from giving him a ration of shit for leaving me alone and thus, by his absence, contributing to the taboo which resulted in one hell of a firefight. To add misery to the whole thing, we all knew that Parks was with the boom-boom girls back at Sin City while the rest of us were getting our asses shot off.

Lt. Barret directed Parks, Houser, and me, to move out to an area between where the Platoon would be spending the night and the rock pile and set up a listening post. We worked our way to within a couple hundred yards of the rock pile, where we located an outcropping behind which we could dig in and spend the night.

That night, artillery was again continually fired into the enemy position. Artillery rounds were exploding not more than a few hundred yards away from where we lay. We hugged the ground behind our protective rocks as pieces bounced about our position. It was a long night for sure, and as it just so happened, ended the first half of my tour in Vietnam.

The next morning, we were again preparing for yet another assault up the mountain, when word came down that tear gas was going to be dropped on the enemy still holed up in their rock caves. We were provided with gas masks and began our all too familiar advance up the mountain. All that morning, before our advance, the Air Force dropped 500 and 1000 lb. Bombs turning rocks to rubble. What we were now experiencing was more of a mopping-up operation than the pitched battle experienced the previous days. As it turned out the majority of the encircled NVA had escaped our net the previous night, leaving behind several innocent porters who had been forced into service from surrounding villages, together with their dead and severely wounded.

Again, it was big-hearted Irving who led the way back to morality. While searching one of the larger caves, a wounded NVA was located so far back into the cave that one had to belly crawl to reach him. He was in bad shape with a hip and leg wound and suffering from shock. Irving crawled back to where he could reach and help the poor guy out of the hole. Once out, it was obvious that the wounded NVA was nothing more than a kid, in his mid-teens. With gook in arm, Irving brought the poor fellow up to the surface and laid him on a flat area. Somehow the NVA soldier had withstood the effect of his wounds and the tear gas. His only protection from the gas was a cloth wrapped around his face. He pleaded for water, but water was in short supply. No one was willing to give up what little they had, except, of course, Irving. The kid, cradled in Irving's arms and Irving giving up what little water he had left to this poor hurt kid, strongly impacted me at the time, and remembering it now reinforces my feelings of just what a good man Irving was. Strangely, Irving was what remained of my other self, showing me that humanity could exist even in war-torn Vietnam. Irving was a special sort of guy. Thank God there are, even in war zones, those special people like him. In short order a medevac was flown in and the poor kid flown out. Word came back that, thanks to Irving, he survived.

So, went the Battle of the Rock Pile. Before it was over, we suffered what I believe to be four G.I.s making the supreme sacrifice, and several others were wounded. Damage inflicted upon the enemy, unknown. Most of the guys were by this time exhausted, and our uniforms were in tatters. My pants were ripped and torn, and my shirt was completely gone leaving me with only a stretched-out t-shirt. We were covered with dirt and grime, but then we always were. An interesting side note on this whole affair was that the gooks had been using the downhill side of several of the rocks we had to climb over as their latrine. I guess Charlie had the last laugh on us. We were eventually airlifted to LZ Pony for a couple of days of rest, night bunker guard, night ambushes and day patrolling.

TROUBLE WITH MESS HALL SARGENT AT LZ PONY

Aug 21ˢᵗ Hangover this morning. No clothes yet.

Aug 22ˢᵗ Got resupplied today. Cleaned up & went to S.F. (Special Forces Camp) for a few (too many) beers.

Aug 23ʳᵈ Patrol today. Left at 7:30 back at 2:30. Looking for VC who kidnapped some people. Actually just moved out and sat.

Aug 24ᵗʰ (New Medic) Supposed to look for VC who kidnapped a girl & then look for a VC – in actuality just moved out & set up. Back by 2:30 at Pony.

Aug 25ᵗʰ Rained all day. We stayed at Pony. LZ Uplift & Ollie both got mortared during the night. Ollie unhurt. Uplift our Blt. got hit. Expecting to get hit.

Aug 26ᵗʰ Co is supposed to move (from) here at noon. Then we are going on a screening mission.

Aug 27ᵗʰ Walked out of Pony after supper. Set up for night in a village moved out and were put on call—hold up. On call all day —nothing.

The morning of April 19th, we air assaulted into an area suspected to be holding the fleeing NVA. Finding nothing we were then flown to LZ Pony, where immediately upon our arrival, and prior to us having a chance to clean up, we were directed to a tent mess hall for our first hot meal in some time. There were no replacement uniforms available for us, so it was a go-as-you-were-affair. For me, I had only an undershirt, and my pants were in shreds. The crotch of my friend Vogal's pants was completely ripped out from leg to leg, and he had no shirt at all. So, there we stood in this artillery mess hall line awaiting our due reward. When, out of the blue, the mess hall sergeant in charge started raising hell claiming we were disrespecting his chow hall. Evidently, he took exception to our general state of dress and our unwashed condition.

Every now and again, it was good to have an officer around. Several of ours, along with our Top Sergeant descended upon this poor fellow and explained the facts to him. "These troops have just been in a four-day firefight during which a number were killed and wounded; now, by God, these boys are going to be fed. NOW!" This resulted in having the whole company moved to the head of the chow line. We were the first to be served. Fortunately, we were able to wash up prior to our next meal, but replacement uniforms didn't show up for a couple of days. The mess hall sergeant made no further remarks as to our attire.

During our stay at LZ Pony, I had the opportunity to walk up to a Special Forces command bunker which housed one of their medics. Another soldier from my platoon and I were to have their medic (*who was highly trained, more so than our platoon medics*) treat a couple of ailments. My friend had a huge splinter, about the size of a short 10-penny nail straight up into his elbow, while I had shrapnel in my shoulder resulting from the friendly fire encounter a few days prior. The idea was to have these removed. My friend was first to go under the knife with me to follow. I watched as the medic took out a syringe with a huge, long needle and proceeded to inject Novocain into my companion's elbow. The pressure of the Novocain eventually forced out the splinter. After watching this procedure and giving it some thought, I concluded that the shrapnel in my shoulder had found a good, safe home where it could reside for the rest of my life. Yes, caution is a tried and true form of valor. The shrapnel didn't hurt, the procedure for its removal would have. Letting it stay where it was, was a no brainer. I did stick around and drink beer the rest of the day with my new, Special Forces, friends. This again resulted in yet another throbbing headache the next morning.

Aug 28th (Bill and Stephanie's Anniversary) Moved out early and climbed over a big mountain. Set up for night on other side. Plt. went on ambush—rained all night. SOAKED.

Aug 29th Moved to new location this morning. Rested, 2nd Plt. made light contact. Night ambush. Called in from ambush at 10pm LZ Uplift was supposed to get hit. We will air assault in support if they do get hit. We air assaulted into Tiger Mts. in the morning.

Aug 30th Air assaulted into LZ Scott in Tiger Mts. Expected Blt. & Reg CP. $100,000 of ordinance was dropped in. Moved from LZ downhill, it started to rain, held up. Moved out again after rain & made contact. Moved back uphill. A Co. seriously hit. BOOM.

While moving down the mountain the 1st and 3rdd Plts. ran into each other resulting in a small firefight taking place before it was realized that we were shooting at each other.

Aug 31st Moved back down the hill. Found a cave with BoCo stuff: mortar, sight, compass, etc. Found bunkers. Moved down to valley. Hard Hump.

Sept 1st Started looking for Plt. CP where A Co. made contact. Found enemy position & 3rd Plt. Moved back to cave found yesterday. Demo team repelled in & blew it up. Humped back to LZ Scott.

Sept 2nd Air assault. Found a large cave complex and blew it up. Set up early with new type of perimeter. (Star-shaped.)

Upon moving down the mountain from LZ Scott on the 30th we ran into Charlie holed up in a large cave and a small firefight ensued. A gunship (*helicopter armed with rockets*) was called in for support. They were able to fire a cable guided rocket directly into the cave which temporarily shut down enemy fire. While the helicopter was engaging, we resumed our assault, and in short order found ourselves standing in the cave entrance. In addition to finding a few deceased NVA we also discovered various NVA items, which were mostly destroyed by the rocket.

The next morning, we returned to the cave and undertook an extensive search. Quite a bit of North Vietnamese gear including a large mortar was discovered. A soldier assigned to an Engineering Co. was flown by chopper into the area but was unable to land, forcing the engineer to repel from the chopper. While this is something we often did, the idea of sliding down the dangling rope scared the hell out of the engineer. It took quite a bit of encouragement before he made the leap. Upon reaching land, he went ahead and blew up the cave including all the North Vietnamese gear except the mortar, which we were told had to be carried back to LZ Scott. I remember the mortar was quite heavy, and we had a long walk before setting up for the evening. It was a hard hump, made especially so by the heavy weight of the mortar.

Sept 3rd Lt. Birthday. Patrolled a draw. Neg finding. Kept same FOB.
Sept 4th Moved our FOB down further into the valley. 3rd Plt. Split from Co. into a draw & checked it out. Nothing. Went on Plt. ambush that night. Ran into LRRPs & set up booby trap. Moved back to Co. in morning.

On the night of September 3rd, a young soldier named Gladding joined me in my fox hole while pulling night guard at about two or three in the morning. He wanted to talk to me about a problem he had with his new wife. They had married just days before he left for

Vietnam. As mentioned earlier, some of the younger soldiers often confided in me and sought my advice on personal problems. Unfortunately, this young fellow was killed shortly after I was sent back to the States. In later years I was able to locate his young wife and relay to her my conversation with her former husband. In doing so I was able to reassure her of his love. She later remarried a boy from my Platoon who was also her former husband's best friend. Unfortunately, this young fellow suffered greatly, and was never able to get the horror of Vietnam out of his mind and was eventually committed to a mental facility. The marriage suffered and finally failed.

"NOT EVERYONE WHO LOST HIS LIFE IN VIETNAM
DIED THERE. NOT EVERYONE WHO CAME HOME FROM
VIETNAM EVER LEFT THERE."

On the late afternoon of the 4th, we were about to move into a draw when the point man heard voices coming our way. We quickly set up an ambush from which maximum firepower could be unleashed upon the source of the voices now almost upon us. I recall lying on the bank of a small stream awaiting the arrival of the enemy. Then, most unexpectedly, we discovered the voices were not Charlie, but those of a U.S. LRRP patrol, who, being oblivious to our presence, had unwittingly stumbled into us. This patrol had a couple of Vietnamese on point, who would have been the first people we would see, and thus triggering the ambush. The only thing that prevented this was our recognizing that English was occasionally being spoken by the U.S. troops making up part of the patrol. The LRRPs indicated that they had not been briefed regarding friendly troops operating in the area. Things like this should never have happened, but they did, and people got hurt. In this case, we came close to wiping out one of our LRRP patrols. They remained with us that night and were flown out the next morning.

CENTRAL VIETNAM AMPHIBIOUS ASSAULT

Sept 5th Secured mortars. Put hammock in tree. Extracted at 2 to beach. Swam in ocean. At 2a.m. made an amphibious assault onto beach in Tiger Mtns.

Sept 6th First man off boat in Amphibious Assault. Walked until about 5:30a.m. then sat on trail until about 6:30a.m. Walked through village & set up on hill. Searched village & walked back to coast.

Sept 7th Moved our FOB towards the base of Mts. Walked up the draws and found a vacant VC village bunker complex. Blew all the bunkers. Sign of very recent activity. Moved down to the new FOB & set up for the night.

Sept 8th Went down into village near coast. Gave out food & medical care. Went swimming in the ocean all afternoon. Evening sat around and BSed.

Sept 9th Air assaulted to top of mountain & walked back to FOB Found trail from top-down. Moved the FOB. Set up ambush. Missed 3 VCs. Lay around on beach today. Barbecue today. Ambush that night in?

On the afternoon of September 6^{th,} we were called upon to set up for receiving helicopters that would be taking us over to the coast. As always, we all looked forward to this, knowing full well it wouldn't be long before we would be swimming in the South China Sea.

We swam in the sea whenever we had a chance. The way this would work is while one squad was in the water, the remaining two would provide security. In this manner, each squad would have its turn to clean up in the water.

However, this time, things didn't quite work out that way. We did go swimming, but no sooner than we were out of the water, were we informed that we were to make one of the few sea to land amphibious assaults undertaken in central Vietnam during the War.

The weather had quickly changed from sunny to clouds then to rain. The rain was preceded by a cold high wind that chilled us to the bone. As usual, we got soaked. Our mission included assaulting into a village by sea, something we had never done, and fully expected the worst. The village was a few miles north of our location and surrounded by high mountains, which made a surprise landing or air assault impossible. The only way to get in there without being noticed was an amphibious assault by sea. We, unfortunately, drew the short straw. Mongoose Bravo would be leading the planned predawn strike into what was suspected to be a large force of NVA. A good day was about to go bad.

There, over the dull blue-gray horizon, was a line of landing craft coming to pick us up and deliver us into what? We didn't know. Expectations were low. Now came the time for us to worry, waiting for crafts to land on our patch of sand. Once the craft reached shore, we loaded, cramming the entire platoon, shoulder to shoulder, into one craft. Again, we pulled the short straw and were to take the lead, or point, upon reaching shore. The rain was now coming down in a torrent, blocking any light from the moon or stars. It was as black as ink, and you literally could not see your hand in front of your face. It was one of the darkest nights that I can recall during my tour in Vietnam.

The Lieutenant, Big Skinny, arranged the troops so that he and I were located at the very front of the craft; thus, we would be the first off once we reached land. As mentioned, there was a cold wind blowing and that, coupled by the spray of the ocean, added to our misery. What surprised me was that the craft was not watertight, resulting in our standing in water above our knees. At some point, I lowered myself onto my haunches to escape the cold wind. Seeing me waist-deep in water the Lieutenant asked what the heck I was doing.

"Well Skinny, the wind is colder than the ocean."

"Oh!" was all he said. Once in the boat, the expectation of my being hurt or killed subsided, and I was at inner peace. I had, over the years, watched numerous WWII movies where young soldiers were in this same situation that I now found myself. What were they thinking? What was their mental state? Were they scared? I remember finding this memory very interesting. I was not frightened. Were they? The memory passed and I gave no further thought concerning the unknown. What would be, would be, and I would somehow survive.

It was well past midnight when our little boat reversed course and headed for land, with us hitting the beach with an unexpected thud. All those aboard fell forward, resulting in one of the troops breaking his arm. Down went the ramp, and we waded ashore, fully expecting to see fireworks, green tracers, and hearing loud booms. But to our surprise, all was quiet, and we stumbled onto the sandy beach. There was no light to aid us in gathering our bearings; all we could do was feel our way, moving north, staying on sand, while paralleling the ocean to our right. It didn't take long to realize that we had no idea where in the hell we were, or where the target village was located. The Company Commander finally called a halt and formed a line on the beach. After about an hour he ordered Lt. Barret to send a squad on ahead to find the village. Myself, along with the radio or because of it, Parks and a couple more moved out into the blackness of the night, continuing at a very slow northern pace; keeping sand underfoot and the sea to the right. After a short time, and still unable to see a foot in front of us, we came to a halt, forming a tight circle and waited for the sun to shed some light by which we could get an idea as to our location and that of the elusive village.

In what seemed to be fifteen or twenty minutes, we started hearing dogs barking and the rustle of women preparing their morning cooking fires. The ink-black night sky yielded to a dull gray. Rain continued to fall. All we could do was stay put and wait for dawn's light. Gradually the outline of huts with thatched roofs silhouetted the morning sky. Women could be seen scurrying about. Some of which were not more than twenty to thirty yards from where we hugged mother earth. Yet we remained unobserved. Somehow without knowing we had walked smack dab into the middle of the target village. Now we fully expected to be discovered and a war to erupt, a war we knew we could not win. We, therefore, beat a hasty retreat, crawling until we were out of earshot. Big Skinny was contacted. We informed him that the company was no more than a click or two (click = 1,000 meters) from its intended target, and for the company to continue moving on its northern path. Parks, myself and the rest of our little squad found some cover and waited for the company to walk by. Eventually, the company did emerge and walked into the village without a shot being fired. If the bad guys were ever there, they had vacated the area sometime earlier.

Finding nothing to shoot at, we eventually took our leave and walked up into the mountains where we set up for the night. We, unfortunately, weren't especially nice to the villagers during our short stay. Orders were to search the village for any sign of enemy activity, and question as to where all the village men were. To this, the response was always the same, "Oh, no Papasan, no Papasan." It was very apparent that several of the women that had gathered were pregnant, while others were carrying small infants. Papasan had obviously been there.

We were not exactly making friends. They had no recourse but to stand by as we entered and ransacked their homes, scattering their meager possessions. During the first six months of my tour, we often

"Zippoed" their homes. Zippoing referred to taking out a Zippo lighter and lighting up their thatched roofs. We did it without remorse. Zippoing was called to a halt during the second half of my time in-country. Fortunately for them, the searching of this suspected enemy village took place in the second half of my tour thereby saving their homes from destruction.

Later the following day we learned that this poor village was continually harassed by both South and North Vietnamese armies. Each side drafting or conscripting the male members of military age, thus explaining the absences of males in the village. Early the next morning, we were ordered back into the village and attempted to make amends by handing out food, household goods such as soap and providing medical attention to those in need. This would be our home for the next few days. It didn't take long for the villagers to relax and start interacting with us. The kids, who always warmed up first, joined us as we swam in the South China Sea. The women brought their kids to the medics to be checked out. As you can see by some of the scars on these beautiful young children, the war had been unkind. War can be hell, but hurting children was the worst. On the 11th we were extracted back to LZ Ollie.

FUN DAY IN BỒNG SƠN

Sept 11ᵗʰ Left for Ollie about 11 am. Took over same bunkers as in July. Got hair cut from gook and drank beer.
Sept 12ᵗʰ Drank beer at gook stand. Laid around.
Sept 13ᵗʰ General coming to inspect artillery today. G.I. got poisoned today from rice wine or coke.
Sept 14ᵗʰ Went on patrol today. Stayed at a hooch. Mamasan standing bare-chested had biggest, well-shaped boobs I've seen in a long time. AMAZING.
Sept 15ᵗʰ Went to Two Bits to BS with Army Photographer. Then to the town of Bồng Sơn. There Tairl, Everhart & I went to whore-house & drank beer & BSed. Then took steam bath.

A main forward base by the name of Two Bits was located next to the town of Bồng Sơn. Bồng Sơn was the equivalent of a County Seat and was the same town that Parks and I visited following my return to the Company back in late July. It was a somewhat peaceful place; although I wouldn't have wanted to spend a night alone there. But on this day, we were at peace with the world—all was good. A couple of days earlier the Platoon walked into LZ Ollie (*approximately 7 miles South of Bồng Sơn on Hwy 1*) and learned that we would be spending a few days there, doing little more than sending out day patrols, nightly ambushes, and pulling night bunker guard. Good work when you could get it.

Spending time at an artillery base such as LZ Ollie was common the second half of my tour. I would assume the purpose of this was to give us a break, a rest, together with a chance to clean up and get resupplied. This is in direct contrast to my first six months in-country, during which we saw very little of civilized surroundings and the relative security offered by these bases. Landing Zones, such as LZ Ollie, offered dug in bunkers surrounded by sandbags and barb wire.

On our second day at Ollie our interpreter, a member of the South Vietnamese Army assigned to the Mongoose, who was from the Bồng Sơn area, decided he would be going to town to visit with relatives. He had earlier lost his mother and father, who were well-educated teachers, and were evidently assassinated by the Viet Cong for no other reason than being educated and well-respected leaders of their village. His story was not uncommon. I recall him leaving his M16 rifle behind and tucking a U.S. 1911, A1 pistol in his waistband where it was covered by his shirt. Evidently, he was not quite sure as to what type of reception to expect.

On the fifth day of our stay at Ollie, with nothing assigned to do, Parks, Everhart and myself decided that we would catch a ride to the hamlet of Bồng Sơn, which was to the north of Ollie. Highway 1 ran north and south inland from the coast and was only a short distance from the artillery base. We planned to stop a bus, climb aboard, and hitch a ride. This we did, climbing onto the buss's roof, which we shared with sacks of charcoal. There we sat high in the sky, wind in our faces, and off to a new adventure.

After riding for what seemed way too long, we decided to halt the bus and climb off and reconsider our situation. We weren't exactly sure where we were. The reality of our situation finally made it through our thick skulls. We were alone in hostile territory without any means to call for help. Dumb, dumb, dumb! How did we get ourselves into this predicament, and how were we going to get out of it? It so happened that we unloaded on to a small bridge, which spanned a creek flowing a small amount of water. There we stood, looking at smoke rising from the mountainside paralleling the road some five hundred meters to the east. Was this from locals collecting and making charcoal or was it something more sinister; smoke from morning cooking fires of North Vietnamese soldiers? Logic suggested that it was the charcoal gatherers, but we weren't sure, and the longer we stood there, the more we were convinced it was the latter. If so, they surely saw us just standing there.

Our immediate plan was to stop anything going south and return to Ollie; unfortunately, nothing was traveling on the road. So, there we waited, watching what we had now convinced ourselves was cook-fire smoke. But whose? We knew we were screwed. All we could do was hope for someone to come by and get us out of the predicament we had gotten ourselves into. There on the horizon, just coming into view was a jeep traveling south at a high rate of speed. It looked to be carrying an officer and driver—but they weren't U.S. Soldiers; instead, they were Asian, either Korean or Vietnamese. Finally, we were catching a break, for if it were a U.S. Officer, we would be subjected to discipline for sure. The powers to be would not understand our desire to skip off to Bông Sơn. No—all hell would come our way. But this wasn't a U.S. Jeep. Thank God.

The jeep continued its approach, quickly narrowing the distance between us. Surely those in the jeep could see us standing there, trying to wave them down. But they just kept coming, showing no sign of slowing. To our dismay, they turned off from the road vacating the bridge and plunging through the small creek and returning to the road on the other side. Leaving us standing in awe as they passed us by. What the hell just happened? They must have thought the bridge was mined, and we were stationed there to prevent oncoming traffic from using it. There we stood with our mouths open, believing evil things were about to happen. As in most cases, the prediction of doom is overstated, and eventually a small Vietnamese civilian sampan came by heading north towards Bồng Sơn which we forced to a halt, climbed aboard and continued our journey. Was it all worth it? Damn right it was! We had one hell of a good time once we finally made it to our destination.

LRRP Mission with a Strange Ending.

On this extended LRRP mission, Parks, Little, Hauser, Vogal, possibly a few more, and I, worked our way up to the top of a mountain overlooking a river valley approximately one-half mile way. There we would stay for the next few days. By the sixth day we, unfortunately, were out of water. Little, a colored kid from the Bronx, was really hurting and getting desperate. What made it all the harder was that from our mountain hiding place, we could observe our target river and the water flowing within its banks. Little was determined to go down to that river the coming night and refill canteens. The rest of us objected to this idea, but Little's mind was made-up. During this argument, a radio call came in, informing us that we would be extracted the next morning and for us to descend to the river at first morning light. With this information, we were able to dissuade Little from going on his misguided, self-directed mission of filling canteens.

On this, our last night on the mountain, while I was pulling one of the hour-plus guard duties, I heard something crawling through the underbrush towards our position. Crack, crinkle, rustle, rustle, the sounds were getting louder with each passing minute. Whatever it was, it appeared to be getting closer and closer. "Oh shit; we've had it. Charlie knows we're here and is closing in on our position." WHAT TO DO! I kept still, listening; trying to ascertain exactly how close to us they were getting. I knew from experience that it would be unwise to fire my M16 and thus giving away our position. The only thing to do was sit and wait and consider options. Not being sure what or how many were closing upon us, I finally decided that best course of action was to throw a grenade to where the sound of movement was coming from. I reached down, took out a grenade, pulled the pin that secured the firing mechanism, commonly referred to as the spoon, and prepared for the throw. My thought was that the sound of the exploding grenade would wake my sleeping comrades, and we could then beat a hasty retreat. Yet I waited, not knowing for sure what, or how many were now just a few yards below our hiding place. There I sat, live grenade in hand, pin pulled; all that remained was for me to throw, grab the night scope and run like hell. All it would take is to give it a toss, thus allowing the spoon to fly off and four seconds later, BOOM.

WAIT a second, the rattling in the brush now sounded more like an animal rummaging through our discarded empty C-rations and other accumulated garbage. YES, that's what it is, just rats savaging our garbage. Now what to do? The grenade in my hand was alive; the safety pin removed and thrown away. Tossing the grenade was not an option. The sound of it exploding would surely expose our position, and we would then really be in deep shit. SO, I just sat there, live grenade in hand, feeling quite stupid.

Parks was, unfortunately, next in line to relieve me from guard duty. When my time was up, I moved over to where Parks was stretched out. "Parks wake up, it's your turn."

"OK Mac."

"Oh, by the way, Parks, here, take hold of this grenade. It's live, and the pin has been pulled—don't let it go; or for God sake, don't doze off and drop it. If you do it will be the last thing you ever do."

"OH SHIT! Mac, what'd you do?"

The grenade was thus passed to each of the following guys as they took over guard duty. I suffered abuse from all, each in turn, had to hold that grenade throughout his turn on guard., making me not a very popular boy. Fortunately, memories are short, and I was soon allowed to rejoin the fraternity. OK, think on the bright side, I'm quite sure that no one went to sleep on guard duty that night.

The next morning before descending the mountain I took a

length of parachute cord, which I always carried, and wrapped it around the grenade securing the spoon in place, then placed it in an ammo pouch attached to my web belt There it would safely stay for the time being. Two days later, while walking through a village, I dropped it down a well. BOOM, the episode of the grenade was over, and things returned to normal, SSDD or better yet SNAFU.

There Really are Elephants in Vietnam

Once again, we were operating in the An Lộc Valley, a noted trouble place. We had spent the previous night at the overrun and abandoned LZ Bird; a spooky place indeed. 1st Cav Soldiers had died there some months earlier. The next day took us to a new and unfamiliar area. I can't recall its exact location, but it was made up of abandoned villages and encroaching jungle. We were informed to be on extreme alert, for the area was suspected of harboring North Vietnamese forces and Viet Cong partisans. That evening we set up with the rest of the Company. One of the platoons was then sent out to create a platoon size ambush some five hundred meters to our right flank. Once settled in for the evening artillery was called in and fired into predetermined locations which would later be used as a point of reference should we get into trouble during the night. The same was set up for the platoon out on ambush. That evening First Sergeant Denison (Top) joined the Company. Over the course of the year, Top had become a close friend to both Parks and I, and it didn't take long for Top to join us for C ration coffee. The question on many minds I am sure was, "What do those two have on Top?" You've got to understand the Top Sergeant is big smoke in the Company. Young Lieutenants cower in his presence. No one, and I mean no one wants to get on Top's bad side. He can bring a lot of heat. Someone you wanted on your side. He saved me more than once on getting my knuckles rapped. Sometimes both Parks and I did push the envelope.

Along about two in the morning, word came in over the radio from the platoon out on ambush that they had movement to their front. The alert went up throughout the rest of the Company. Now we waited. What was probing the ambush position? If shooting did erupt, we would most certainly be committed to the fray, or conversely, would they hit us? Wait, Wait, nerves on edge, but no word from the platoon on ambush. Finally, they were back on the radio informing the Company Commander that the movement previously mentioned now appeared to be elephants. "Elephants, you got to be kidding?" was the Company Commander's response. We knew that elephants were in Vietnam and used by the NVA to move their supplies and heavy weapons. Was this the case, or where they just wild elephants native to the area? No way to know, so the decision was made to fire artillery into the general location of the last observed elephant. BOOM, BOOM, a battery unloaded into the suspected area. All quiet, no more elephants. We settled into what was to become an uneventful night except of course for the elephant encounter. Early the next morning, my platoon, the 3rd took up the point, hot on the trail left by the departed beasts. They headed straight into heavy jungle. No blood, just a trail left by overturned trees and brush. They just walked through the jungle, paying no heed to the brush and other tangles; just walked through it all. We followed them for the better part of the day, but never overtook them. Eventually, we gave up, ending our pursuit and set up for another night in the wonders of Vietnam. Elephants, you really got to be kidding!

Abandoned on Top of a Mountain

This, like the recollection of the elephants, took part in the last third of my tour. For some reason, I make no mention of these events in my journal. It was not uncommon for me to leave extended periods of time unrecorded. Why? I don't know. But, eventually, for no known reason, I would start writing again.

We had been operating on the coast, west of LZ Ollie, when out of the blue, word came in over the radio to form a large LZ, one that could accommodate enough choppers to lift the entire platoon at one time. We were to be flown out in one sortie and join the rest of the Company, which was located on a mountain top quite some distance from our current location.

While we were waiting for the helicopters to arrive one of the new guys informed the Lieutenant, he wasn't going. This was new, I'd never seen one take this approach for getting out of the field. The Lieutenant, who was standing next to me, proceeded to explain to this guy in no uncertain terms, he was either going or facing a court-martial. At that point the guy did something very stupid, he lowered and pointed his M16 at the Lieutenant. Seeing this, I lowered my M16 and shoved it against the chest of the now quite frightened soldier. This resulted in the now visibly shaken young fellow lowering this rifle. Situation resolved; he didn't accompany us that day or any other day. He was just gone. I didn't see this guy again for several months; when I came upon him serving in supply shortly before my returning home. Would I have shot him? Probably...Yea? He would have got himself killed if he would have taken off the safety on his M16. But now, thinking back on it and having the incident washed by time, I'm not sure. No, I would have shot him, no doubt. Then, life was cheap, and I was hard. Shooting him was not outside of something I could do. I was still roaming the forests west of the Cumberland Gap although the beast within was now somewhat tamed, but it was still alive and well.

I've never been able to absolutely identify the mountain we landed on. No maps of the area were made available. All I remember is that we were on top of a tall mountain surrounded by equally tall mountains somewhere east of the Bồng Sơn plains and west of the Cambodian border. I also believe we were quite a ways north of An Khê. I guess it was secret, secret stuff, for no maps were provided. Upon landing, we scattered, forming a defendable perimeter. Once security was established, the Lieutenant dispatched a small group of us to proceed down a well-used trail immediately to our front and straddling the mountain ridgeline. When no more than a few hundred meters down the trail, word came over the radio for us to get back with the rest of the Company. This was unusual; the trail obviously presented a potential danger and should be explored. That was SOP, but not this time. For some unknown reason, we were just to hold a loose perimeter securing the mountain top and ridgeline. Shortly following our return to the Platoon, the sky was again full of helicopters flying in a battery of 105s (*Artillery*). Now it made sense, we were part of an artillery raid. The idea was to fly in artillery, place it well into enemy-held territory thus bringing the artillery within range of the suspected NVA position. The guns opened up and continued firing throughout the remainder of the day. However, during this whole time the powers to be didn't want us to form a tight secure perimeter. We were directed not to dig in or send out patrols or even established listening posts forward of our position. This was definitely out of the ordinary, strange, very strange.

Late in the afternoon, the weather started to turn, the wind picked up, and an occasional rain squall would settle in. Again, the sky was loaded with choppers. Cables were dropped and the 105s attached then lifted and hauled away. This was repeated again and again until all the artillery was extracted. Next, choppers came in for the troops, pulling them off the mountain top. The weather continued turning nasty, winds picking up and rain becoming heavier. One by one, the men were extracted; platoon, by platoon. We were the last in line. Despite the changing weather each member of my platoon was evacuated, all except Parks, I believe Houser, a kid by the name of Ronny and myself. It was not uncommon for me to be among the last to be lifted out of an area due to my keeping ground radio contact with the extracting Slicks (helicopters). Several attempts were made to extract us; however, each attempt was thwarted by the deteriorating weather. Again, and again, a helicopter would try to land, but to no avail. It appeared we were about to be on our own until the storm let up. This could reach well into the next day and even then, we may be required to find another place to complete the extraction. I wasn't unduly alarmed; we could walk out if need be.

One thing was for sure, Charlie would assume the artillery was still on the mountain top and would be sending in soldiers to investigate. In the process, all he would find would be four lonely 1ˢᵗ Cav troops. No, we could not stay where we were, or bad things would happen. But no word came for us to start walking; we just sat there, alone, wet and cold. Evening was fading into nightfall, and we still waited on word on what we were to do; stay or walk. Our, or should I say my preferred option was to start walking and find a place to be extracted the next day.

The wind was whipping over the ridge top, first from one direction then another. Little daylight remained. I was getting nervous. We couldn't stay where we were, but no word came for us to pack up and find another home for the evening. One thing was obvious to all, Charlie was on his way. No, we had to get off that mountain and find a new hole to crawl into. Then out of the sky comes yet another chopper. It tried and retried to land, but the wind continued moving him from one side of the ridge to the other. The pilot encouraged me to stay put, he would get us out. All I can do is keep him informed as to where he is in relation to the ground. Finally, a shaky touchdown and us scrambling aboard, and then off into the rainy evening.

We landed in a broad field where the rest of the Company had set up for the night. It was no more than three or four miles from the mountain upon which we had been stranded. The meadow in which we now found ourselves was covered with knee-high grass and devoid of trees. Because we were late in joining the Company, most of the work of digging in and setting up a night defense was already finished. Unfortunately, so was partaking in eating any of the hot dinner meal that had previously been flown in. Another evening meal of Cs for us. Along about midnight all hell broke loose with the blowing up of the mountain top we had just departed. B52s were unloading hundreds of 1,000-pound bombs on our previous location. The bombs were so powerful that even though we were a considerable distance away the concussion from their blast rocked us. This went on for some time, then all quiet for the remainder of the night. The next day we were flown to yet another area from which we would undertake a new day's trek through yet another village and rice field of the Bồng Sơn Valley.

The Rest of the Story of our Near Abandonment on the Mountain Top

It just so happens that on February 11th, 1968, just a week before my going home, Parks and I were at the Battalion NCO Club in An Khê, enjoying a beer before retiring for the night. Shortly upon entering the club, First Sergeant Dennison spots us and insists on buying a round of beer. Conversation ensues about all that has transpired over the last year when the First Sergeant asks if we were ever informed as to what took place the evening we were stranded on that mountain top. As the story goes, a large encampment (Battalion + in size) of NVA was in the valley immediately at the foot of the mountain upon which the artillery had landed. A plan was devised to entice this large force to a single location; i.e., the mountain top, where we could blow the hell out of them. So, the bait was the large number of artillery pieces that were flown in and sitting on that mountain. The belief being that the NVA could not pass up such an easy target. This explained why we were not to send out patrols and why we were not to dig in. We, together with the artillery were bait, a sacrificial pawn, that would be extracted at the last moment. An unanticipated consequence arose when the powers from above found themselves with four of their soldiers stranded upon the intended target of a B52 air raid. They believed that it was too late for the stranded soldiers to avoid the anticipated large blast area. Likewise, even if they were somehow able to get enough distance from the target, they probably would be unable to evade the large number of anticipated enemy soldiers ascending upon them. There goes the best laid plans of men and mice—the unanticipated consequence. Four stranded soldiers were not part of the planning.

Finally, a decision was made to abandon us and continue with the B52 strike, and thus condemning us to certain death. Yes, just sacrificial infantry ground pounders on the chessboard of war. It was this lone slick (*helicopter*) pilot who wouldn't give up on us. He knew our fate if abandoned. He just tried and kept on trying, risking his own life to get us off that damn mountain. Parks, Everhart, Houser and I owe that truly brave, yet unknown pilot our lives. If he had not made that last attempt to extract us, we would surely have met our fate that night.

R AND R MEETING JAN IN HAWAII

Sept 16th Went on a local patrol today. Donut Dollies (Girls with the USO) came out for chow.

Sept 17th Went to LZ Uplift (our battalion head courters) Got shots & new clothes. Left for An Khê and R&R with Bunch.

Sept 18th Went to Town today (Dad's birthday). Ended up in Sin City. Pulled Plt. CQ that night.

Sept 19th Went to town with Curtis.

Sept 21st R&R leave An Khê Went to Cam Ranh Bay. Went to EM Club that night.

Sept 22nd Leave Vietnam for Hawaii. Met Jan. She is completely dominating my life.

Sept 24th Shoulder pain Same shoulder with grenade frag.

Sept 25th Went to Tripler Army Base beach.

Sept 27th Went to Hospital.

Sept 28th Left Hawaii for Cam Ranh (Vietnam).

Sept 30th Arrive back in An Khê.

R and R, or more precisely, a week of Rest and Recuperation in a country far from the war was the promise made to each soldier in Vietnam. More often, we soldiers referred to it as *I & I*, or Intoxication and Intercourse. It was the subject of many foxhole stories. What you'd do on *I & I*, and a whopper of a story would follow by the soldier who recently returned. For me, it was a week in Hawaii with my wife, Jan.

R & R began with my departing An Khê on the 21st of September for Cam Ranh Bay, and then to Honolulu, arriving on the 22nd. I checked into our hotel ahead of Jan and immediately took a real shower in a real bathroom and then fell asleep on a real bed for the first time in nearly nine months. It felt great. Jan awoke me on her arrival, and that's as far as I'll go on that.

We spent our time on the beaches and touring the island in a rental car. I guess I still had my California Driver's license, but then I know I didn't carry it while in Vietnam. At one point, while driving next to the ocean, I observed a wave come into shore and exploding over a rock shelf. It did not repeat the explosion with every advance; instead a short lapse in time would occur before repeating itself. I stopped the car and told Jan I wanted to take her picture standing on this rock with the ocean as a backdrop. She had no idea that the rock I was asking her to stand on periodically got drenched, so off she goes and with a big smile stands for the picture. I take one shot of her before the big surprise and one just after. You be the judge. She was pissed, but a good sport. I thought it was hilarious.

Our week in Honolulu was over far too soon. Unfortunately, shortly after my arrival, my shoulder, the one with the grenade shrapnel, started to bother me. In short order, the pain elevated to the point of needing medical attention. I ended up in Triplet Army Hospital with the doctors trying to decide what to do. First off, they needed x-rays. So, off to the x-ray room I go. The waiting room was a rectangle of approximately 20' by 30' with a wooden bench running along its sides. Upon entering, I discovered that all of the seating was occupied by pregnant girls who were staring at me as though they had just caught the rooster in the hen house. After turning a few shades of red I remarked, "No ladies, I'm not," meaning pregnant of course. They got it, and laughter erupted in the waiting room. The doctors never could decide on what to do, so they took the easy out and sent me on my way back to Vietnam with a slip of paper to give to sickbay once back in An Khê.

Finally, it was time for us to part. This parting was the hardest for me of all the separations we incurred while serving in the military. I didn't want to say goodbye and go back to war. All I wanted to do was go home, but as before "go, I did."

PUNJI STAKE WOUND: SECOND PURPLE HEART

*Oct 13*th *Start NCO School.*
*Oct 22*nd *Got punji stake in right leg while operating just north of the pass.*
*Oct 23*rd *Medevacked to An Khê. Operated on and put in hospital.*
*Oct 24*th *Transferred to Quin Nhon.*
*Oct 25*th *Operated on again.*

Immediately upon returning to An Khê following R&R, I was sent to sickbay and remained on light duty for the following week. While there, I received orders, indicating I was to attend NCO (*Non-Commissioned Officer*) School. I guess it was an honor to be picked, but I wasn't excited about attending. The carrot offered to entice you to give it your best was that the person who finished first in the class would be promoted to his next rank. This was interesting because my orders promoting me to Buck Sargent, E-5 were already in the works. Did that mean should I lead the class upon its completion that I would completely skip the rank of E-5 and go straight to SSG E-6— Staff Sergeant? Don't know because I was wounded three days before the conclusion of the class and never finished it. At the time, I was one of the top three in the class. I really had a good shot at winning it. That would have really been something, go on R&R as a Spec 4 (E-4) and come back to the Company as a Staff Sergeant (E-6). I guess I'll never know.

The school was made up of approximately 20 to 30 infantry soldiers, with training in Army discipline and infantry tactics as its primary function. In addition, we were available to be used as a reactionary force in reserve, available for insertion as needed. The final exam involved a field exercise in which each soldier is ranked on his implementation of the material learned in class as well as his leadership skills.

Our field exercise was to serve two purposes; implementing skills learned in class, while the other of a more practical nature involved locating and eliminating a 50 Cal machine gun and its crew harassing both planes and helicopters approaching An Khê. The gun location was somewhere in the higher mountains on the north side Highway 17 as it crossed the An Khê Pass.

Upon landing in the suspect area, it was discovered we were smack dab in the middle of a field of punji stakes. Fortunately, no one was hurt while jumping from the chopper. A punji stake is a long bamboo strip sharpened to a razor's edge and a pinpoint. It is no more than a foot to a foot and half in length and about 3/8 of an inch wide. It is planted into the ground where it is concealed by high grass and brush. They are quite lethal, and during my tour in Vietnam, several our boys found themselves being impaled in the leg by a punji stake. This resulted in a deep, highly infectious wound. The infectious part is due to the stakes often being dipped in human dung before planting. You get stuck with it as you walk by, brushing up against the stake and having it penetrate your leg. The wound is usually quite deep, and because of the possibility of it being infused with dung, it is considered a severe injury; one requiring the removal of all flesh that came in contact with the punji leaving a hole an inch or so in diameter and as deep as the punji penetrated. No fun, a real ouch.

Upon landing and after addressing the punji situation, a Command Post was formed and patrols sent out; each patrol was led by one of the students from the class. It was soon my turn to lead a patrol and off we went. Things went well until the point man signaled back that he was encountering punjis. The column was halted while the lead element cleared the trail. With the punjis now posing a minimal threat, we continued with our assigned mission—find the harassing machine gun and destroy it and its crew. The patrol advanced no more than twenty to thirty yards before I walked into a punji hidden in a bush. It pierced deep into my right leg just above the top of my boot. Without thinking about it, I reached down and pulled out the stake and gave in a heft down into a ravine running parallel to the trail we were using. Mistake, for I knew that when stuck by a punji, keep the stake for the doctors treating the wound, and the opportunity to examine it for human waste. If not contaminated the medical treatment is quite simple. He just sews up the wound; however, if soiled with poop it becomes much more complicated. Unfortunately, I did throw the stake and thus condemned myself to invasive surgery.

Some of the boys of the patrol said that they would go down into the ravine and try to retrieve the punji. This offer I refused. The possibility of having one of them also stuck by a punji was just too high. The stake must have hit an artery, for the bleeding was heavy. Now, the immediate problem was to stop the bleeding that was pumping from the wound, and then call in a medevac for extraction back to the hospital in An Khê. Fortunately, applying pressure got the bleeding under control, not stopped but under control; so off we went.

Immediately upon arriving at the hospital, I was sent to an operating room and prepared for surgery. From past fox hole discussion on the treatment of a punji wound, I knew that a circular plug would be extracted from where the punji entered my leg and would follow it until all flesh impacted by the wound was extracted. In my case, the wound was quite deep, passing my leg bone on its way to the other side. The excised area thus being a plug of about one inch in diameter and about 3 to 3.5 inches long. I was fully awake during the entire procedure and conversing with the surgeon as he addressed the wound. At one point I asked, "How deep is it?"

His response, "Feel that, well that's your leg bone, and the punji found its way past it into the other side." The whole operation lasted no more than a half-hour, followed by being assigned a bed in a recovery ward. The strange thing about this is I never suffered much pain.

This resulted in being awarded my second Purple Heart, which was important because there was a time-honored rule in my unit that no soldier would be put back on the line after receiving his second Purple Heart. This rule was strictly enforced by our First Sargent. It was a taboo; if sent back out the soldier would surely receive a fatal wound and thus put a curse on the rest of the unit.

There will be no thirds! No, never. Threes of any kind are taboo, bad luck. That's the rule. I told you we were superstitious.

A couple of days later found me being transferred to a major hospital in Quin Nhon where I underwent an additional operation. In the bunk next to me was a helicopter crew chief who had been shot in the ass, piercing both cheeks. One gets no respect when suffering an ass wound. There's simply no glory in it. "In the ass, you got to be kidding me?" There's just no respect. The obvious question that always follows is, "How's the pain in your ass?" You get the picture. Regardless of Forest Gump—there's just no glory in an ass wound. We kidded the hell out of this poor fellow. Actually, ass wounds are quite painful, and my new-found friend was hurting. My wound, at this point, was still open, unstitched. The idea was to have it heal from the inside out. However, this practice significantly increased the chance of infection; therefore, one had to be closely watched. Interestingly, my previous gunshot wound in the neck, which on its own could have been life-threatening, was nowhere as involved as this wound. Eventually, I was flown to Cam Ranh Bay, back to the recovery hospital I was in following my neck wound.

While in Cam Ranh I was assigned to an intensive care ward, which really amounted to nothing more, as far as I could tell, than being restricted to the ward and not having to get up to go to the mess hall for your chow. It would be brought to you on a tray. Eventually, my leg was stitched up, using a small gauge stainless steel wire. Shortly, after that, I was kicked out of the intensive care unit and reassigned to a ward. Now I had to get my own chow.

The mess hall was a large barrack-like structure feeding the entire hospital. Noon, on my first day out of intensive care, I tackled the long line and enjoyed lunch sitting at a table. This was quickly consumed. After which, for some unknown reason, I just continued to sit and observe the long chow line. How could they possibly feed so many people?

I looked up, and down the line studying the soldiers as they approached, then, out of the blue, I observed what looked like a familiar face. I got up and walked over to this soldier. As I got closer, his facial feature became clearer. "My God, that's Parks." Can you believe it? Together again and in short order assigned to the same ward. Yes, we worked it out so that we bunked next to one another. He had come down with malaria and was just now recovering. He was thin, bent over, withdrawn, and white as a sheet. All in all, he looked like shit. We spent the better part of a month enjoying the sandy beach of Cam Ranh Bay.

After about three weeks I left Parks and bid my farewell to Cam Ranh Bay, rejoining my Company in An Khê. Upon arrival, First Sargent Dennison sought me out and informed me that there would be no THIRDS and asked where I wanted to be reassigned for the remaining two months of my tour. In response, I indicated I would prefer to be assigned to somewhere I could still be a benefit to the Mongoose (*B. Co, 1/5 Cav*). This resulted in being assigned to forward supply. Ask any soldier it's always good to have a friend in supply. My new job was overseeing the final loading of resupply helicopters destined for units out fighting the war. This assignment gave me the opportunity to assure that the Mongoose got the supplies it needed. If there was a shortage, the Mongoose would now be first in line.

Eventually, Parks was released from the hospital, and on his return to the Company, Sargent Dennison informed him that his younger brother, Tex had arrived in Vietnam and was also assigned to the 1st Cav. Dennison made it clear that he would not have two brothers serving in the infantry and both assigned to the Cav. Thus, Parks was asked, "Where do you want to go." His response, "Where's Mac?" and he too was assigned to the same forward supply unit. We were again rejoined.

In early December, our battalion was called back to An Khê, from where we would be located for a couple of weeks. While here, Park's brother came for a visit. I have no idea as to why we decided that we needed a shower hot water heater. But we had observed the construction of such a unit utilizing a mess hall garbage can heater and pump. It looked as though we could make one of these ourselves. The idea of a hot shower was quite compelling. Mess hall can-heaters are readily available, all we needed was a pump. One was observed in the area of an adjacent engineering unit. A plan was devised where Tex, together with another fellow assigned to supply, should, under the cover of darkness, sneak over to this engineering unit and relieve them of their pump. So, that night, after consuming way too many beers, our Watergate burglar unit prepared to undertake their mission. BAD IDEA, they were caught and were held in the day room of the engineering unit waiting to be released to a couple of Sergeants from Tex's unit. As it turned out, both sergeants at the time had already started on a bender. Upon arriving at the engineer's day room, they assured the MPs holding our burglars that strict disciplinary action would be enforced. With this assurance, they were released to the Sergeants.

The two boys sat in back of the jeep as the two sergeants continued to improve on their drunken state. "Damn, you boys can't even steal a simple pump. What the hell are you thinking? Let us show you how it's done." Then the two Sergeants proceeded to go back and steal the very same pump. Following this, both boys were driven back and released to me. No discipline followed. Unfortunately, the two sergeants kept the pump and built their own shower heater.

Eventually, my portion of the 1st Cav. was assigned to relieve the

Marines up in I Core, along the DMZ. This resulted in our finally moving the entire supply unit up through Hue with orders to take Hwy 1 to Quang Tri where we would find our new home. Our route to Quang Tri had us driving past Hue the morning of the day of Tet. Our orders were to make it to our destination before 7 p.m. or stop in place and remain there while the annual Tet truce was observed. Well, we all know that truce never happened, and in short order the Tet Offensive was underway. By mid-afternoon with us still on the Highway, new orders came down for us to not stop for any reason and make it to Quang Tri. That night, after reaching our destination the Tet Offensive was on in full force, and Quang Tri was under attack. Two weeks later both Parks and I were on our way home.

Status of the second Purple Heart

Now, as for the second Purple Heart, its paperwork never caught up with me; however, the actual medal was awarded by my Company shortly before going home. I was on my way to the next hospital when the officer responsible for completing the necessary paperwork attempted to locate me at the first hospital I was sent to. Unfortunately, he never was able to run me down. I later learned about this from some of the other soldiers who shared the same ward I was in at the first hospital. I really didn't care at the time about all this. It just wasn't important to me. The officers of the Mongoose and First Sergeant Denison knew that I had earned it, and that was all that mattered at the time. I have given some thought over the years about having this properly awarded. Captain Hugh Forrester, a former Company Commander of the Mongoose has discussed this with me. He said he could get it awarded and attached to a revised DD 214. I understand the VFW, of which I am a member, also helps straighten things like this out. Well maybe someday, but it's not now high on the priority list. It's strange, the VA has it listed as a service-connected punji stake wound. Where did they get the info?

THE HOLIDAY SEASON 1967

I t's now the beginning of the holiday season (November 2018) as I sit here thinking back about the season of 1967. I really can't recall much about it. For starters, just before Thanksgiving, the unit was back in An Khê. So, I must have had Thanksgiving there. I'm sure the mess halls were turning out turkey dinners with all the trimming, but I just can't remember. For me, it was just another day in Disney Land. What I do recall is it was about this time that Jan's father, George Trotter, sent to our Base Camp, Camp Radcliff, in An Khê thousands of Christmas tree lights and the making for a huge wire Christmas tree. This was erected on the tip-top of Hong Cong mountain that overlooks the entire Base Camp area. There it stood for all to see. A huge lit-up tree sent to the First Cav. by my father-in-law. It was quite the talk of the town, and I was quite proud to tell all who sent it.

Sometime right before Christmas, we were sent back to LZ Uplift located in the heart of Bồng Sơn Plains and shoot-um-up country. Here Parks and I spent our days leading up to Christmas. Again, don't recall much other than First Sargent Dennison and the Sargent Major asking if I wanted to share the tent that was erected for them. I took this to mean that they wanted me to set up sandbags around the tent. I was quite busy at the time and told Dennison I didn't have time to make the move. Much to my surprise, he informed me that he already had my few possessions moved in and that the sandbags were already in place. I really felt quite honored and touched by the offer and subsequent moving of me into their quarters. Here was I, a new Buck Sargent moving in with the top-ranking Sergeants of the Battalion. It must have created some heartburn by other higher-ranking sergeants who were not asked to share the quarters. I loved it.

The scuttlebutt was quite ramped at the time that the Cav. was being gathered up for a major move. Our destination was believed to be the invasion of the north and taking of Hanoi. Of course, the Cav. would be in on such a move. As usual, the scuttlebutt was wrong, or should I say only half right. A major move was in the making. We were headed for I Corps and the DMZ to assist the Marines.

As for Christmas itself, it was spent at a new location just south of Hue, Phu Bai. I don't recall anything special about Christmas while here. We must have had a good meal. Our mission when we arrived was to set up a new Base Camp to which we would be relocated. The area selected for this was right next to this massive South Vietnamese graveyard. How Appropriate! During the Christmas season, the USO was providing numerous shows at the major installations. Of course, Bob Hope was the main attraction. Somehow the Army forgot to invite us. So again, Christmas was just another day. A day of which I have no recollection at all.

Shortly after New Year's, we were again on the move, up to Camp Carol and Quang Tri; just in time to be caught on the road during the start of the Tet Offensive. So, ended my holiday season of 1967 in Vietnam.

Letter to Bill Simmons:

This letter offers a window into my thoughts upon hearing about the political strife occurring in the States in the late '60s and '70s.

December 15ᵀᴴ

Well, I am getting down there. I'm getting too short to even get up in the morning, much less walk around scheming. You know, I think that our intelligence is finally getting somewhere. If S-2 sends it down that Charlie is down in the valleys, we hump the mountains, and if they say he is up in the hills, we go and harass the low villages.

You know even the literature seems to be changing. A person finding himself with only a matter of days to go, reads, "10 telltale signs of a cheating wife," "The flower movement talking over the USA," "Black Revolt 68" and all other good-sounding news. Gee, I can't wait to get back on the good old safe city streets in the U.S. I've even heard that the life expectancy of a man walking alone after midnight downtown San Fran is 5 min (REALLY?) You know that's really heartwarming. The nightwalker is 3 min safer than a point man here. Now really less than 3 minutes[1]

Hey Old Buddy, I did get assigned to Fort Ord. Therefore, it looks as though that winery will make it out of the red in '68. I should be home anytime from Feb 13-20ᵗʰ, then I will get a 30-day leave.

See you in Feb,
Tim

---

1. *This is an important addition to this paper. While the numbers used here are used in jest, it shows just what our troops were hearing, and thinking about. We really didn't understand the why for all the problems back home. We fully realized that there would be no welcome wagon celebrating our return*

BACK IN THE WORLD FEBRUARY 19, 1968

I t was finally time for Parks and me to say our goodbye to Vietnam and go home. We had survived our one-year vacation in Southeast Asia. The route home was via Cam Ranh Bay to McChord Airbase Washington State. From there on to Fort Louis Washington, the very place where both Parks and I started our military careers.

This was the plan, but as usual, something went wrong. On route our plane suffered mechanical problems while refueling in Okinawa, Japan, which resulted in a day-and-a-half layover. A group of about four of us took this opportunity to explore the area, meaning find a bar, of course. The only advice given before our departure was, *"Stay out of Four Corners."*

It didn't take too long to locate a respectable night club where we settled in until closing time. Now, what to do? We still had three or four hours before we had to be back at the airport. The bartender indicated that there were a couple of after-hour clubs and that he could arrange for a cab and notify the after-hour club of our pending arrival. Sounded good to us—Let's Go. We soon learned we were headed for four corners; where else? The taxi driver took us down this long, dark back street, eventually stopping, getting out, and informing us he would arrange entrance to the club. Things were not looking good! Down the street was a gang consisting of seven or eight tough looking men, gathering and heading our way. It was obvious that we were set up and bad things were about to happen. The taxi driver however made a big mistake. The keys to the cab were still in the ignition. I simply slid over, started the cab and made our departure. We eventually reached a major road where we abandoned our cab and flagged down another. Eventually, we made it back to the airport—where we would stay put until departing on our flight home.

Fort Louis, Washington, was eventually reached, and new uniforms and a big steak dinner awaited us on our arrival. From here, a bus to the Seattle Tacoma Airport was provided. This would be Park's and my point of separation; with me being assigned to the 51st Infantry out of Fort Ord, Monterrey, California, and Parks to Fort Sam Houston, Texas.

With time to kill while awaiting our respective flights, we settled down in the lounge with the intent to order one last beer together before we said our final good-byes. Another soldier who had served with us in Vietnam by the name of Louis joined us at the bar and a round of beer was ordered for all. To our surprise, the bartender indicated he couldn't serve our colleague, Louis. He was underage —we had no idea; not giving Louis's age any consideration. The bartender apologized profusely, knowing that our friend was on his way home after serving his year in Vietnam. Upon hearing this from the bartender and assuring him that we did understand, I ordered two beers for myself. The bartender indicated that would be OK, and thus Louis got his beer. I guess he was old enough to fight and perhaps die in Vietnam but wasn't old enough to share a beer with friends. GO FIGURE! I truly believe any man wearing a CIB on his chest is old enough to have a beer anywhere he Damn Well Pleases.

From here Parks and I said our goodbye and assured one another we would meet again. Which we did and have maintained a close friendship over the ensuing fifty-plus years. I spent the remainder of my active duty with the 51st Infantry leaving the Army in June 1968.

My final separation from the military took place on September 7th, 1971, six years to the day following my induction into the Army.

Parks eventually found his way back to California, where he started a new life with a wonderful new bride. We remained in close contact until each took on a new job. Me, working for Central California District located in Los Banos, California, and Parks leaving his job with Hollow Tree Lumber and moving back to Texas. Unfortunately, we failed to notify one another about these moves and thus lost contact.

Some ten years later found me attending a conference at State Line, on the California, Nevada border. With nothing particular to do following the last speaker for the day, I decided to take a walk. The sidewalk was quite crowded, and my idea was to separate from them as soon as possible. As the crowd thinned, I observed a fellow some distance ahead with a familiar gait to his walk. I closed the gap between us until I was immediately behind this guy, thereupon I shouted, "Parks, you son-of-a-bitch." To Parks these were fighting words, and he abruptly turned, "God Dam Mac, it's you." We've remained close ever since, often visiting one another. No two brothers could ever be closer than Parks and myself.

Life goes on and with it, the locked-up memory of an old man. Did all this actually take place as here indicated? I believe, or should I say I hope so. In the end and after much soul searching; was it all worth it? HELL NO! Either way now that this is complete, I can finally say

"GOOD BY VIETNAM."

ACKNOWLEDGMENTS

There are numerous people who have had a part in this undertaking, far too many to list here. Probably first and foremost it's time to recognize those all too often forgotten brothers in arms who actually carried the rifles and fought the Vietnam War; especially those I walked with, in the valleys, villages, and mountains of the central coast of Vietnam during 1967 and 68; those brave, all to young members of the Mongoose Bravo, 1/5th, 1st Cavalry, who were called upon to give up their youth in the service of their country. A partial list must include, but definitely not limited to:

Tairl Parks, Ronny Everhart, Doug Curtis, Docimo, Boharkas, Dave Irvine, Buzzy Suman, Ron Douchene, Jones, Greco, Storie, Eddleman, Ron Houser and Platoon Leaders Lt's. Waggner and Barrett and Platoon Sergeants Vieth and Allen, and Company Top Sgt Dennison...They will live forever within my memory of Vietnam.

The front cover depicts a sitting soldier. This was taken from a personal photo of the California Vietnam Memorial located in Sacramento. I would like to acknowledge and thank Col. Hugh Foster for his tireless effort in keeping the unit together over all these years and for providing me with official records of events that transpired during 67/68, including the record of the Battle of June 21st.

I reference within the body of this work the historical significance of Cumberland Gap as discussed by Fennimore Cooper in his "Red Stocking Tales" and the digression of man as he crossed this famous landmark separating the eastern seaboard and the internal wilderness of the Tennessee Valley during the 1700s. I found this to be a simile of how we, as soldiers lost much of our humanity while fighting the war.

Finally, this work could not have been brought to completion without the editing help of Griffin Smith, who tackled the ominous task of editing and putting into book form the final product. Without Griffin, this work would have remained as a Word Document, stored and forgotten, floating somewhere in the Cloud.

ALSO BY WAR HISTORY JOURNALS

WORLD AT WAR: UNFORGETTABLE TALES FROM THE FIRST AND SECOND WORLD WARS

"True Stories of Endurance, Horror and Beautiful Human Beings." – Reviewer

Haunting Truths We Must Never Forget.

Follow in the footsteps of the British, German and American servicemen as they detail the life and struggles of war in mysterious and foreign countries. Uncover their mesmerizing, realistic stories of combat, courage, and distress in readable and balanced stories told from the front lines.

This book brings you firsthand accounts of combat and brotherhood, of captivity and redemption, and the aftermath of wars that left no community unscathed in the world. These stories have everything from spies and snipers to submarines and air raids. A great book for anyone who wants to learn what it was like during the world war conflicts between 1914-1945.

BROKEN WINGS: WWI FIGHTER ACE'S STORY OF ESCAPE AND SURVIVAL

"A masterfully told story of triumph and redemption in a powerfully drawn survival epic." – Reviewer

Hero WWI Fighter Pilot Shot Down and Captured.

With an engaging and authentic retelling of his experiences as an escaped prisoner of war, this gripping account details the life and struggles of a captured pilot in 1917 war-torn Europe.

Lieutenant John Ryan couldn't wait to see action in WWI. He joined up with the British colors out of Canada. As one of several American pilots in the Royal Flying Corps before the US joined the war, he earned his wings and became an Ace through fierce air battles over the skies of Germany.

WAR ON INFLUENZA 1918: HISTORY, CAUSES AND TREATMENT OF THE WORLD'S MOST LETHAL PANDEMIC

"A remarkable yet frightening history that serves as a stark warning of the threat of pandemic flu." – Reviewer

Influenza Should Scare You.

Read Into this detailed and chilling account of the Influenza outbreak of 1918. A terrifying virus that stretched across the globe. Even now, a century after the great flu of 1918, which left an estimated 50 to 100 million people dead worldwide, there's still no cure.

This book examines influenza from all sorts of angles—history, diagnosis and treatment, economics and epidemiology, health-care policy, and prevention, and it gives insights on pandemics.

Visit us at www.warhistoryjournals.com

Lightning Source UK Ltd.
Milton Keynes UK
UKHW010627020622
403888UK00001B/128